PRESCRIPTIONS for HAPPINESS
To Use and Give to Others

℞

A variety of Prescriptions
that can keep you happier,
healthier and reduce
your pills and doctor bills
and
heal broken hearts and lives

By
Jack C. Kelley

Copyright ©1999 Rx for Happiness
By Jack C. Kelley

All rights reserved. Printed in the United States of America
For information:
Cameron Graphics, Inc.
14199 SW Millikan Way
Beaverton, OR 97005
ISBN 0-9658046-1-5

Grateful acknowledgments for
Editorial Assistance:

Sherri Ladislas

Elizabeth Macy

Doris Wheeler

Anne Kelley

Dedication

This book is dedicated to my wife, Anne, for her love, patience and encouragement. Without her, this book would not have been possible.

ABOUT THE AUTHOR

Jack C. Kelley is a free lance writer and author. He is a licensed pilot and served in the U.S. Navy.

The Prescriptions for Happiness in this book have been published in newspapers and periodicals. Through these, Jack hopes to make a difference in this world by getting people to return to the basics of plain ol' common sense and decency. This, in turn, will make for more caring and happy people and even a safer world. These prescriptions are easy to take. They will give you encouragement, joy and put a smile in your heart and on your face. They are not preachy, but helpful and spiced with humor. They can turn your sad days into glad days.

Kousin Zeke sez:

"To make your world
and this world happier,
safer and better,
use dabs of Common Sense"

Jack Kelley
Alias "Kousin Zeke"

CONTENTS

TITLE	PAGE
✔ Check this box when you share an article with someone	
❑ Carry Smiles	1
❑ Troubles Galore	2
❑ It Could Be Worse	3
❑ Mr. Mule	4
❑ Don't Carry Fear	5
❑ A Lemon Family	6
❑ A Good or Rotten Day	7
❑ Twenty Four Hours To Practice	8
❑ Building a Life-House	9
❑ Check It	10
❑ How To Make Decision	11
❑ Bury Pride	12
❑ Don't Miss The Little Things	13
❑ Telling Big Tales	14
❑ Fume, Fuss, Fret	15
❑ A Watermelon Patch	16
❑ Tender Loving Hugs	17
❑ Hate Mosquitoes	18
❑ Bona Fide Flu	19
❑ Jelly Bean Prayer	20
❑ Do You Have Enough Money?	21
❑ What The World Needs	22
❑ Stealing – A Self Check	23
❑ Missing Some Bricks	24
❑ Find Buried Treasures	25
❑ Dumb Excuses	26
❑ Best Beat Spouses	27
❑ Encouragement	28
❑ Ten Suggestions	29
❑ Why The Fourth of July	30
❑ The Bottle Habit	31
❑ Fixing This Goofed-Up World	32
❑ Santa – A Symbol	33
❑ Three Berries	34
❑ Don't Miss The Basics	35
❑ Better Than The Average Bear	36
❑ Just Don't Do It	37
❑ Grains of Sand	38
❑ Booster Shots	39
❑ The Best In The World	40
❑ Are You A Winner or Loser?	41
❑ What Number To Call	42
❑ How To Make A Difference	43
❑ Four Letters - TGIF	44
❑ Band-Aids Needed	45
❑ Footprints	46
❑ A Good Night's Sleep Is Possible	47

CONTENTS

TITLE	PAGE
✔ Check this box when you share an article with someone	
❏ Who Can You Believe?	48
❏ Get A Dab	49
❏ A Dumb Frog	50
❏ Know Who Is Calling	51
❏ Blank	52
❏ Be Spicy Nice	53
❏ Ings Can Do Us In	54
❏ I Just Took A Pencil	55
❏ Try Courtesy	56
❏ Livid Rage in 10 Seconds	57
❏ Never A Loser Unless You Quit	58
❏ Gossip Ain't No Game	59
❏ The Devil's Beatitudes	60
❏ Right Now!	61
❏ I Love My ?	62
❏ Inside Or Out	63
❏ Joe's Town	64
❏ Just Being Polite	65
❏ No Binoculars On The Titanic	66
❏ Peep In The Box	67
❏ Happy Habits	68
❏ WWJD	69
❏ Don't Ask Me	70
❏ Kids' Talk	71
❏ I Ain't Addicted	72
❏ Don't Let Your 4th Be A 5th	73
❏ Just Miss It	74
❏ Squash The Bugs	75
❏ Is God Black or White?	76
❏ Depression	77
❏ Good or Gooder	78
❏ Just For Fun	79
❏ Wits-End	80
❏ Clock Strikes 13 Times	81
❏ Do you have HS?	82
❏ Grade Yourself	83
❏ Hypocrites	84
❏ Be A Plus and Not a Minus	85
❏ Prescription For Happiness	86
❏ Our Goof-Ups	87
❏ He's No Fool	88
❏ They Are Not Lost	89
❏ What's Your Definition of Happiness?	90
❏ "Enthusiasm"– Do You Have It?	91
❏ Coping With Agitators	92
❏ Anxiety	93
❏ Happiness Is A Choice	94

INTRODUCTION

How do you rate your happiness? Choose one grade.

😁	Dazzled	❏ A
🙂	Pleased	❏ B
😐	Neutral	❏ C
☹️	Annoyed/Upset	❏ D
😠	Infuriated	❏ F

Which of the above faces do you wear? Only you can choose which face to wear. I enjoy being with contented happy people. What about you? We each face daily battles with pride, selfishness and wrong decisions, but we can win out over life with enthusiasm, confidence and inward peace. God can't change our face but he can change our heart. If we permit him to change our heart, then our heart will reflect smiles of joy.

Let me share a suggestion with you. Most of us would like to have happy pills. I can't give you happy pills, but this book contains PRESCRIPTIONS for HAPPINESS. The pages are PERFORATED so that you can share the prescriptions with others. You can run off copies and give them to lots of folks. What can the prescriptions prevent or cure? Worry, guilt, anxiety, fears, pride, jealousy, hate, prejudice, gossip, depression, stress, divorce, lying, stealing, drug and alcohol abuse, addictions and plain ol' sins.

Even better, these PRESCRIPTIONS can reduce your PILLS and doctor BILLS. There are no monthly payments; no yearly checkups, no insurance requirements, no age limit and no batteries are needed. IF TAKEN AS PRESCRIBED, we will be healthier and happier.

When should we begin using these PRESCRIPTIONS? Begin today, please, please do not delay until tomorrow. Take time to care, and be a ray of hope to those in their darkest hours. As Kousin Zeke would say, "Regardless how much you and I are hurtin', there is someone else hurtin' worser. If we have faith and use dabs of COMMON SENSE we can't lose. People don't give a hoot what we know, if they know that we care. That is the reason and purpose for this book.

CARRY SMILES

What do you carry around with you every day of your life? Most of us carry some type of identification. We carry billfolds, purses, credit cards, keys, pencils and just plain old stuff. What's the most necessary, essential thing you and I lug around?

Let me share with you something that I learned from an attractive young lady, a cashier in a large department store. Did I ask her what she carried around every day? No, but she explained to me what she carried, after I made a comment. As I was waiting in line to pay for my purchase, I noticed how busy she was in the midst of customer confusion yet, she continued to smile as if it were routine. As I paid for my purchase, I remarked about her beautiful smile. This was her comment, **"THANK YOU, I TAKE MY SMILE EVERYWHERE I GO."** She did take her smile everywhere but she also left it with others. How did I know? When I left, her smile was still radiating in my heart and I was thankful for the joy she smiled on me.

Kousin Zeke sezs, "We better be doubly cautious what's we tote 'round every day, 'cause the ol' devil don't take no vacations. He wants us to tote 'round **the three G's**, **GRIPES**, **GROUCHES** and **GRUMBLES**. When we tote around the three G's, it ain't too long 'til we become **BELLYACHERS**, **SOURPUSSES** and **COMPLAINERS**." My advice to you and me, realize life ain't too complicated if we listen to our hearts. The beautiful cashier had learned the secret to happiness, tote around God's love-smiles in our hearts and his love will splash on others.

TROUBLES GALORE

Do you ever think, I've got more **TROUBLES** than Job. Let me tell you about a lady who almost had more **TROUBLES** than Job. This lady was traveling on a train with her children. A man sitting nearby began telling her his **TROUBLES**. Her small baby was screaming at the top of his voice and the man said, "Lady can't you stop that baby from crying, with all my **TROUBLES** he's about to run me crazy?" She said, "You think you got **TROUBLES**. Listen sir, See that girl over there, that's my daughter, she's expecting a baby any minute and she ain't even married. My husband is in the baggage car, we're taking him to be buried. That baby sitting next to you has messed in her pants and her small brother has chewed up and swallowed our train tickets."

TROUBLES can be like sleeping on a mattress. We can sleep on top or under the mattress but common sense says it is preferable to sleep on the top. As long as we live on this earth we will have trials and worries. The choice is ours, we can bury **TROUBLES** or permit **TROUBLES** to bury us. It is not always easy but it can be done. Kousin Zeke sez, "Over 2000 years ago Paul gave us some good advice. Always be full of joy. Don't worry about anything. Pray about everything. Tell God about your **TROUBLES**. Give your **TROUBLES** to him. Don't forget to thank him. If you do this his peace will keep your thoughts and heart quiet and at rest as you trust in Christ."

Maybe the lady on the train should have written this article. When we begin our pity parties she would say, "Wake up and smell the roses, you ain't got it so bad after all."

℞ IT COULD BE WORSE

Regardless of how deplorable her situation, Susie Q always replied, **IT COULD BE WORSE**. She had some so-called friends who resented her happy attitude. They were jealous and looked forward to the day when she could not possibly say, **"IT COULD BE WORSE."** The incident finally occurred. Susie Q's husband had run off with another woman and left her with five kids. Believing that this was their best opportunity to gloat, the ladies paid her a visit. One of the ladies said, "We heard that you were deserted by your husband and wondered what you will do now." Susie Q replied, **"IT COULD BE WORSE."** This statement shook up the women and they all responded, "How could it be any worse?" Susie Q said, **"HE COULD COME BACK."**

These women, like thousands of people, enjoy living under the plague of **DOOM** and **GLOOM**, spiced with **JEALOUSY**. Everyone has a choice. There is a saying, **"MISERY LOVES COMPANY."** These ladies were miserable and jealous that Susie Q was not miserable. Jealousy will, if we permit it, **KNOCK US DOWN** and then **SPIT ON US**. Kousin Zeke sez, "Don't let **JEALOUSY** win out. The ladies kept their eyes on others and Susie Q kept her eyes on the Good Lord. The best way to kick the **JEALOUSY HABIT**, do like Susie Q, keep looking up and say only what we know is good and right. Then **JEALOUSY** will slip out of our vocabulary and, **IT COULD BE WORSE**, can slip in.

MR. MULE

The story is told of a small child that went to visit her grandparents who lived in the country. The little girl had never seen a mule and as she was walking behind the barn she saw a mule with long ears and a drooping face. The girl said, "Mr. Mule you must be related to some members of my family. They never smile either." Does it ever pass through your mind what other people see when they look at your facial expression? I'm not referring to the times when we get all prettied up in front of a mirror. I'm talking about the face we wear every day at home, work and play.

Kousin Zeke sez, "Many of us have an uppity opinion of ourselves and often when we think we are pleasant and obliging we are meaner than the devil himself. I takes my 'vice from King Solomon who said thousands of years ago. 'A happy face means a glad heart.' Jesus is my cardiologist."

Here is your **SELF-HELP FACIAL CHECKLIST**. Do your own grading, are you?
- ❏ Happy   ❏ Cheerful   ❏ Glad   ❏ Mad
- ❏ Sad   ❏ Frowning   ❏ Hateful   ❏ Griping

Let's make a difference in this world. How? **Wear a SMILEY FACE daily at work and play.** And hey! Don t forget to take it home to your family. Maybe your dog will like you better.

℞ DON'T CARRY FEAR

What's something that we transport daily? We lug it to bed, wake up with and carry it everywhere? It affects us like being in a darkened tunnel with no exits and a hungry lion on each end looking for a meal. It's **FEAR**. How does fear express itself? Through useless worry, our minds churning non-stop, feeling of helplessness, panic attacks and mood swings. What can trigger these **FEARS**? Facing the unknown, family problems, finances, drugs, alcohol, no faith, weak faith, can't forgive, hate, selfishness, plain ol' greed or doing what we know is wrong (sin).

Kousin Zeke sez, "If some **FEAR** is clobbering you, I knows it ain't no fun time, 'cause **FEARS** can knock you down and spit on you. Then we begin to ask ourselves, is there an answer, will I ever have peace of mind or even survive? I tells you, there is an answer and peace can be yours."

We can learn from David who was overwhelmed by a multitude of problems, sins and fears. What did he do? "He asked God to take away all his fears." Guess what? David found the peace he sought. The same peace of mind is promised to you and me according to Psalm 34:4. If some fear is lambasting you and you have a fearful heart in the darkest of moments, then read verse four over and over, memorize the verse and let its promises be yours. Let's make this a habit each time some **FEAR** pops into our minds and attempts to gain the mastery over us. It does work but the solution is up to us. What's the prescription? Kousin Zeke tells us, "My Lord sez, just don't worry 'bout anything, invite me to run your life and keep 'yo' thanks a'coming."

A LEMON FAMILY

Let me ask you a strange question. If you were standing on your head would you be frowning or smiling? Here's why I ask. Luther Cross wrote a story about the **LEMON FAMILY**. Here is a short run-through of this family. Their names were **GLOOMY, GLUM** and **SNOBBY**. They started a Sunday church school in their home but when the children came they were so unfriendly the children never came back. Father Lemon started an ice cream business but he frowned so much his customers never came back. Nobody liked the Lemon family so they just stayed home, sat in a circle and frowned. Finally Glum got tired of sitting and so he stood on his head. An upside down frown is a smile. So it looked like he was smiling. Father Lemon began to laugh. Mother Lemon began to giggle. They all roared with laughter. Their faces felt so much better that they never frowned again.

A good question to ask ourselves, if we stood on our heads would we be smiling or frowning? Now I ain't telling you to stand on your head 'cause standing on your head has nothing to do with smiling or frowning. What's in our hearts determines our facial expression. Kousin Zeke, sez "The Good Lord tells me to stop **GRIPING and COMPLAINING, BE THANKFUL 'CAUSE ONLY HIS PEACE WILL KEEP OUR HEARTS QUIET AND AT REST AS WE TRUST HIM.** I'm here to tells you, if you is **UPSIDE DOWN** or **DOWNSIDE UP**, if you can muster up even a half a smile at life and others, you can keep a smile on your face.

A GOOD OR ROTTEN DAY

Someone explained how to tell when it's going to be a rotten day. YOU CALL SUICIDE PREVENTION AND THEY PUT YOU ON HOLD. YOUR BIRTHDAY CAKE COLLAPSES FROM THE WEIGHT OF THE CANDLES. YOU SEE A '60 MINUTES' NEWS TEAM WAITING IN YOUR OFFICE, YOU TURN ON THE NEWS AND THEY'RE SHOWING EMERGENCY ROUTES OUT OF THE CITY, YOUR BOSS TELLS YOU NOT TO BOTHER TO TAKE OFF YOUR COAT. YOU CALL YOUR ANSWERING SERVICE AND THEY TELL YOU IT'S NONE OF YOUR BUSINESS. YOUR CAR HORN GETS STUCK ACCIDENTALLY AS YOU FOLLOW A GROUP OF HELL'S ANGELS. THE BIRD SINGING OUTSIDE YOUR WINDOW IS A BUZZARD.

Let me tell you how to know when it's going to be a good day. Remember, the past is over, it's done and I mean gone. We can learn from the past. We only have one second to use at a time, but we can use our seconds for good. Some people live and dwell on the rotten side of life. Those folks complain, criticize and find fault even with Jesus. Realize, we all GOOF-UP but we can't let our GOOF-UPS get us DOWN. That's the problem, when we permit our GOOD DAYS TO TURN INTO ROTTEN DAYS. Kousin Zeke sez, "When I comes 'cross IMPOSSIBLE SITUATIONS and I can't see no LIGHT AT THE END OF THE TUNNEL, I calls on the Good Lord and I sez, 'I'm sorta lost in this tunnel and I need your light for directions.' Guest what? He ain't failed me yet. Now I've failed him but thank God for his forgiveness. Try him out and you can ONLY HAVE A GOOD DAY and the word rotten won't even be in your vocabulary."

℞ TWENTY FOUR HOURS TO PRACTICE

Kousin Zeke asked me an oddball question. He said, Jack ol' buddy, do you knows how to make lots of folks faint? I said, Nope, so what s the catch? Zeke said, Ask them to be polite, say thanks, open doors, be courteous, pass on compliments, let others be first, be nice, clean up their trash mouths and in general act like ladies and gentlemen. Now Jack you knows I'm just exaggerating 'cause this won't make most folks faint. I assure you some people are so rude and thoughtless that if they became congenial and pleasant some of their family members and friends may not faint but they could come close to a heart attack. May the good Lord help 'em".

Someone told me a **THOUGHT** that's a **SURE-ENOUGH PRESCRIPTION: IF YOU WAKE UP WITHOUT A SMILE, REMEMBER YOU HAVE 24 HOURS TO PRACTICE SMILING BEFORE YOU WAKE UP THE NEXT MORNING**.

As Kousin Zeke would say, "Man, that 'am some good 'vice, and for certain it will prevent fainting spells, could cut down on pill taking." What's say we practice lots on smiling? God only knows if we need it, if so let's **PRACTICE** and **PRACTICE**.

℞ BUILDING A LIFE-HOUSE

I heard a strange story about a faithful employee and a generous employer. The employer intended to build a new home but was scheduled to go to Europe for one year. Realizing his employee, William was dependable, he asked him to supervise the entire construction of his new home. He was told to use his own judgment in every phase of the project.

William agreed to build the home but he decided to cut costs and corners and that he did. He used cheaper building materials, for 4x6s he used 4x4s. He even reduced the amount of concrete for the foundation. He thought with a beautiful paint job no one will ever recognize the poor structural quality.

After a year his boss returned. He asked William to take him to see the new home. When they arrived at the location his employer complimented William on the beautiful new home. He then thanked William and said, "I didn't tell you BUT THIS IS YOUR HOME, HERE ARE THE KEYS." Man, that would SHAKE ME UP. What about you? This should be a lesson for everyone. We should think twelve times about the building materials we use in our own LIFE-HOUSE. Do we cut corners with inferior VALUES, MORALS AND ETHICS. Kousin Zeke sez, "We gotta make a choice. We can do like Charlie Brown when he GOOFS UP, he says, GOOD GRIEF or we can say, GOOD LORD forgive me, help me. You be the ARCHITECT and BUILDER of my LIFE-HOUSE.

CHECK IT

A gifted pianist with God-given talent was performing in a competitive concert. The winner would receive the opportunity to play in a concert with the college symphony orchestra. As she began playing she made two mistakes. Immediately her mind began to dwell on her mistakes, so much so that it affected the remainder of her playing. Later she explained to me what occurred and how poorly it made her play. I then shared with her what I had seen on TV. I was watching a football game. The sports announcer was Lindsey Nelson, a renowned broadcaster for many years on TV and radio. As he was broadcasting he made a mistake, goofed-up. What did he do? Did he get upset? No. Did he apologize for his mistake? No. Did he explain his GOOF-UP? No. What did he do? He said, "CHECK IT" and continued to broadcast the game.

We can apply CHECK IT in most parts of daily living. How? For most of us life is a series of GOOF-UPS 'cause we all GOOF-UP at one time or another. If we are not cautious, our GOOF-UPS can STEAL our JOYS, make living one miserable experience. Our GOOF-UPS can keep our minds so cluttered with useless worries that we cannot think or do our best. What can we do with our GOOF-UPS? FORGET them, LEARN from them, and CORRECT them when possible. Kousin Zeke sez, "Thank you Jesus for forgiveness and second chances and then move on with your life as if you ain't never done a GOOF-UP." Get a blessing and give a blessing. Find another GOOF-ER UPPER like you and tell them about CHECK IT.

℞ HOW TO MAKE DECISIONS

HOW TO MAKE DECISIONS. You say, Jack I made a big GOOF-UP, a bad decision . So what, who hasn't. Do you realize, when you stop making mistakes, you will be dead? Be thankful you're still alive and can correct your GOOF-UPS. Kousin Zeke sez, "When we make wrong decisions, it's like riding a sixteen wheeler, going down hill without brakes. Bad decisions don't always kill us but we may wishes we were dead." Most decisions are unimportant but many become enormous problems and often become emotional dilemmas. Fear of making the wrong choice often results in indecision and unhappiness. Everyone must make decisions about: families, friends, neighbors, work associates, schools, jobs, and the future, etc. Make up your own list.

GUIDELINES FOR MAKING DECISIONS: If followed prayerfully and conscientiously will guide you in making good choices.

1. Pray about your dilemma. Ask for guidance.
2. Read the Bible, understand what it says, then do what it says.
3. Talk to mature and trusted friends.
4. THIS IS A MUST - Draw a line down the center of a sheet of paper. Then on either side of the line write down the PROS and CONS. (GOOD and BAD). Be absolutely honest.
5. Let the facts simmer in your mind as long as possible.
6. Make the decision that you believe is best in complete confidence that

    God's will is being done and not yours.
7. Try not to question your decision again. Trust God completely and let him open or close any doors in the future.

BURY PRIDE

Joe said to Leroy, "Leroy, you don't pay your bills. What your friends gonna say when you die?" Leroy said, "The same thing they said about Uncle Peter when he died." What's that? "BURY HIM." Is there more to life than this? Believe me there is. What's your opinion of a murderer, a thief, a liar or someone who is deceitful? It's easy to hate these type of persons and if possible condemn them to hell. Their habits should be condemned. Jesus gave a catalog of all the above sins, BUT, HE ALSO INCLUDED PRIDE. Do you know the meaning of PRIDE? It is BOASTFULLY EXALTING ONESELF ABOVE OTHERS with moral and spiritual insensitivity; in plain 'ol' English it's PREJUDICE. Are we guilty?

Kousin Zeke sez, "For most of us, it's our thinking, thought-life that pollutes our minds and makes us unfit. This ain't nothing to sneeze at 'cause one of these days you and me is gonna stand before our MAKER and I don't want to hear, Kousin Zeke depart from me, I don't know you." Let's each of us remember that life is more than what they said about Uncle Peter, BURY HIM. If PRIDE IS A MAJOR PART OF OUR THINKING, Let's ask for FORGIVENESS, change our THINKING and ATTITUDE-Then BURY PRIDE and PREJUDICE FOREVER. Guess what? You and your dog will be HAPPIER AND SO WILL THIS WORLD.

DON'T MISS THE LITTLE THINGS

Are a bigger house, car, winning the lottery better? Do you believe that bigger is better? I was in Kansas City and read an editorial by Barbara Shelly. This is what she wrote, Don t miss the little things amid the big. Everything in Kansas City is getting bigger and bigger, the nations largest casino opened, it may not be legal but it's big, a mall with 160 stores, an office complex so large it may require it's own Zip Code, a new speedway will wipe out 136 homes, houses with enough bedrooms to qualify as dormitories, drivers are trading in small cars for bigger cars, for minivans and for sports utility vehicles. Mrs. Shelly did not say it's wrong to be big or to have better but she did write, "Don't miss the little things amid the big. So if you are out there driving to get a better computer, in your bigger vehicle, after dining on a more sumptuous meal at a larger restaurant, KEEP AN EYE OUT FOR THE LITTLE THINGS."

Kousin Zeke sez, "It ain't no sin to possess LOTS but the danger is the LOTS may possess us. Me and my family have learned that with LOTS of faith and BIG DABS of love we can possess plenty, whether we have lots or little." Mrs. Shelly closed her editorial with this comment, "Big is big right now. But small is enduring and it is the little things that will console us if our bubble burst." Jesus made a similar comment more than 2000 years ago. "Don't be anxious about tomorrow. God will take care of your tomorrow too. LIVE ONE DAY AT A TIME."

℞ TELLING BIG TALES

Jimmy was a nine-year-old boy that enjoyed telling big tales. His facts became fantasy and he exaggerated beyond belief. This habit became such a problem for his teacher that she spoke to the principal. The principal said, "Ask Jimmy to come to my office and I will tell him a tale he cannot top." When Jimmy came to his office, the principal said, "Jimmy, let me tell you what happened to my family this week. We were having a barbecue in our backyard and a 300-pound bear jumped the fence and began to attack me. I would have been killed except for a small dog that came into the yard and ran the bear off. Can you believe that Jimmy?" He said, "Yes sir, that was my dog and that's the third bear he has run off this week."

Does that tale sound familiar? It should since big tales (lying) for many people is a way of life, especially in advertising. Read a few: THE BEST EVER - VOTED NUMBER ONE - NO CREDIT OR BAD CREDIT YOU CAN BUY IT - YOU CAN'T LOSE - WIN THE LOTTERY - THIS BEERS FOR YOU - THE WORLD'S FINEST.

Kousin Zeke sez, "Lying ain't nothing new. Moses had to remind his people not to lie with the Ten Commandments. DON'T LIE. It don't take a rocket scientist to figger out what's a lie and what ain't. Mama explained to me 'bout lying, with a belt, in the wood shed. I ain't forgot to tell the truth since. One fact I've learned, when we tell one lie, it take dozens more to clear it up. Always tell the truth and there won't be nothing to clear up."

If we have a problem with telling the truth, a trip to Mama's woodshed could help. But even better, ALWAYS let our YES BE YES and our NO'S BE NO.

FUME, FUSS, FRET

Did you ever hear of FFF? Probably not. It used to be if you received an F in school you flunked. It used to be if you were 4F you flunked your physical and could not get into the military. Today if you are a FFFer you won't flunk but your family and friends will pray you do flunk. What in the cotton picken' world is a "FFFer"? It's people who FUME, FUSS and FRET at anyone, anything that bugs or upsets them. A good example are the nuts in traffic. Don't ask a "FFFer" to spell the word PATIENCE, 'cause they don't even use the word. Most of us are guilty and that includes me and I'm working on me.

A sure-enough, bona fide "FFFer" almost believes the world is coming to an end unless the frustrations of life plays to their tune. I will admit the world will play its last tune someday but according to Kousin Zeke, "We better know who we is and where we is going 'cause the world ain't coming to an end simply because someone didn't jump when we hollered." About 90% of the incidents that upset "FFFers" never take place. If you doubt this, keep a record for one month of the happenings that causes you to lose your cool. In other words anything that upsets you. You will be happily surprised.

What's the reward of those who FUME, FUSS and FRET continually? It's FRAYED NERVES, A WRINKLED FACE and A DOWNCAST LOOK. How can we stop losing our cool and making SO MUCH TO-DO OVER NOTHING? Kousin Zeke sez, "The solution ain't no big deal. Don't permit life's daily happenings to become crises. You'll be happier, your family will begin smiling again and maybe your dog will come back home."

℞ A WATERMELON PATCH

A friend of mine showed me his garden. He asked me, "Do you know what s the best plant in my garden? I said, No, but one plant appears to be healthier. He replied with a slightly disgusted smile. While I was planting my vegetable seeds, I was unmindful that my small son was placing WATERMELON SEEDS where I had just planted vegetable seeds! So what do I have now? A few vegetables in the middle of a WATERMELON PATCH."

There are some gardening rules that apply to life: THERE IS A TIME TO PLANT, A TIME TO HARVEST. TAKE CARE, WHAT AND HOW YOU PLANT. WE REAP WHAT WE PLANT. The National Ad-Council broadcast this message on public radio. "No law says you have to FEED THE HUNGRY, GIVE FOOD OR BLANKETS, HELP OR VISIT THE SICK OR SHUT-INS ETC., but 80,000,000 people do this on a regular basis. Over 9,000,000 people in the U.S. are lonely and depressed." You say Jack, "What's that have to do with Me.? If we're not, let's begin planting seeds of love and care for the less fortunate."

Kousin Zeke sez, "I'm gonna plant good and caring seeds, 'cause I wants my Lord to say when I stands in front of him, Zeke, you done some good planting with the LOVE AND CARE SEEDS I gave you. Now, you can live forever in a BEAUTIFUL GARDEN and not in a WATERMELON PATCH."

℞ TENDER LOVING HUGS

Do you ever feel like a lamb, lost in the boondocks, thinking that no one in this world gives a hoot whether you live or die? At one time or another most of us have depressing feelings and often we have no solution. I would like to suggest one possible remedy. Its called (TLH). How can (TLH) provide relief?

Let me share with you what (TLH) did for one person in a counseling session for depression. A friend of mine was part of this session. When the session ended she noticed that one man remained. He was sitting with his head down, despondent and at the point of tears. My friend told me, "I do not go around hugging men but I went over and gave the man a gentle hug. The man looked up and said, Oh God I needed that." This loving hug, completely rekindled this man's attitude. At the next session everyone noticed how the (TLH) so transformed this man's mental anguish that the counseling leader had everyone share a TENDER LOVING HUG before leaving.

What's the benefit of hugging? No batteries, inflation proof, non-fattening, no payments, non-taxable, theft-proof and fully returnable. Kousin Zeke sez, "If you knows someone who needs a touch of God's love, go and share with them a TENDER LOVING HUG. I promises, when you gives a blessing you gets a blessing."

℞ HATE MOSQUITOS

Hate WEEDS, BEEPERS, MOSQUITOS. This statement appeared on a TV network. I couldn't understand why such a statement was shown on TV. Who doesn't hate MOSQUITOS and WEEDS? I didn't understand why we were told to hate WEEDS and MOSQUITOS until the message on the TV said, "BUT DO NOT HATE PEOPLE."

There are a GILLION THINGS PEOPLE HATE. Few kids like spinach, but 'old POPEYE for years has explained how much spinach gave him muscles, so some kids eat spinach. They may not like it but they eat it. Some people hate their neighbors, almost anything that moves, and some things that don't move. How stupid can you get? A book was written explaining how the fans of one university could hate the fans and players of another university. The author included a lot of things to hate. I wasn't born on a turnip truck, so I ain't found nobody that needs to be taught to hate. It just comes naturally. I attended a football game between these two schools. When the opposing team came on the field, I never heard louder booing. I guess that they had read the book. Those fans need to read the good book.

According to the dictionary, HATE is to DETEST, DISLIKE, WISH TO SHUN. Kousin Zeke sez, "Some folks have done caught the HATE VIRUS, don't KNOW NO CURE and DON'T WANT NO CURE. What's the cure? ASK THE GOOD LORD TO FORGIVE YOU-STOP HATING-PRAY FOR THOSE YOU DISLIKE OR HATE. I ain't saying it's as easy as falling off a log, BUT I PROMISE YOU WILL FEEL BETTER, LOOK BETTER AND EVEN SLEEP BETTER."

BONA FIDE FLU

Have you ever had the FLU? I don't mean a bad cold. I mean the bona fide FLU that makes you wonder if you will live and encourages you to pray that you won't. Often I will say to my friends, I haven t seen you lately, where have you been?" They reply, "Oh, I've had the FLU for a few days" or "I've missed two days of work with the FLU." Let me tell you something, "I've only had the FLU two times, I mean the honest to goodness FLU that makes your chin bones knock, your tonsils squeak and you ache from the top of your head to the bottom of your feet." So when some people tell me they had the FLU, I just wonder if they had a fuzzy cold or the real thing. If you know someone who has the FLU, I promise you one thing, they need a shot of cheer and a smile. How can you produce a smile? Give them this article.

> When your back is broke and your eyes are blurred,
> And your chin bones knock and your tongue is furred,
> And your tonsils squeak, and your hair is dry,
> And you're doggone sure that you're gonna die,
> But you're skeered you won't and afraid you will,
> Just drag to bed and have your chill.
> And pray the Lord to see you through,
> Cause you've got the Flu, Boy, you Got the Flu. (copied)

JELLY BEAN PRAYER

Did you ever hear of the JELLY BEAN PRAYER? I never did until I was given one in a plastic bag with 7 JELLY BEANS. You will not find this prayer in the Bible. It is very unique and one of the sweetest prayers anyone could ever pray. I have no idea who wrote this poem but IT CAN TOUCH YOUR HEART STRINGS.

JELLY BEAN PRAYER

RED is for the blood He gave

GREEN is for the grass He made

YELLOW is for the sun so bright

ORANGE is for the edge of night

BLACK is for the sins we made

WHITE is for the grace He gave

PURPLE is for His hour of sorrow

PINK is for our new tomorrow

A bag full of **JELLY BEANS**

COLORFUL and **SWEET**,

Is a prayer - Is **A PROMISE**

IS A SMALL CHILD'S TREAT

The 7 JELLY BEANS in the plastic bag were the same colors as those mentioned in the poem. Pretty neat eh? Make this your TREAT and share this TREAT WITH OTHERS.

DO YOU HAVE ENOUGH MONEY?

A successful businessman asked me a puzzling question. Jack, how do you know when you have enough money?" I said, "I don't know." Was that a good answer? Yep, cause I was employed in his print shop, trying to pay college bills, wondering why a millionaire would want another million. I guess people surmise, if we make two million we'll be richer and happier. I can promise we may be richer but there's no guarantee for happiness, whether we are counting stock dividends or food stamps.

One fact is certain, YOU CAN BE POOR AS A CHURCH MOUSE AND STILL BE SELFISH AND STINGY. Jesus told some selfish followers. "DON'T ALWAYS BE WISHING FOR WHAT YOU DON'T HAVE." He told this story to make his point. A rich farmer had such a harvest he had to build more barns to handle the overflow. Then he said to himself, "Now, I can take it easy, have wine, women and song. But he remembers: Fool! Tonight you will die then, who will get it all?" Kousin Zeke sez, "Man that shakes me up. I better do some RE-ADDING and RE-CHECKING and I mean QUICK."

Do you know how to retain possessions? Give them away. Sounds crazy but it is absolutely true. If you doubt it, ask a generous person who shares with others in their needs. A generous person will have A SMILE IN THEIR HEART AND ON THEIR FACE. Why? It's more BLESSED to GIVE than to GET.

℞ WHAT THE WORLD NEEDS

What do you think this world needs? One song says the world needs love. I totally agree. But Kousin Zeke sez," The world needs something else, almost worser, it's a DAB OF COMMON SENSE DECENCY. Now I don't claim to be the brightest and I ain't got no Ph.D. but I do have a CS degree. Believe me a CS degree is even better." If you doubt what Zeke said, read about some people who goofed up and failed to use COMMON SENSE.

A girl said, "I didn't even think about DRUGS, SEX OR AIDS. I went home with a friend and now I have AIDS."

This was a headline in a major newspaper. "YOUTHS GET 15 YEARS IN STOP-SIGN SLAYINGS." On a drinking and crime spree they stole 19 STREET SIGNS, resulting in the deaths of three teens.

A father molested his own children. The father received what he deserved, DISGRACE and JAIL. He should have gotten the electric chair.

A senior citizen said, "I just took it. I didn't think it was stealing." He's now doing his thinking in jail.

A high school student called in a false bomb threat. His friends said he just made a mistake. His mistake was bad judgment.

Most of us have goofed up big time. Anytime the BIG ME is in charge it spells DOUBLE DISASTER. Kousin Zeke sez, "When I don't knows what to do or zackly what's right or wrong. I sez Lord I needs help, it works. When we practice using DABS OF COMMON SENSE, it can spare us HEAPS of HEADACHES and TEARS."

STEALING
- A SELF CHECK -

Are you a thief? Do you steal paper clips, pencils or cars? Maybe not but there is a world-wide stealing epidemic. Readers Digest had an eye-opening article by Cheryl Downey entitled; Life's Little Larcenies. She included a rogue's gallery of people who steal. 1. **MAGICIANS**: Their motto, NO ONE WILL MISS IT. They steal hotel towels, toilet paper and TVs. 2. **EASY RIDERS**: Their motto, WHO WILL IT HURT? They steal from department stores, dent your car fender and drive off. 3. **PENNY PINCHERS**: Their motto, WHY SHOULD I PAY. They steal from cable TV, income taxes, corporations and their own employers and whoever.

Here is a **SELF-CHECK BAROMETER**, that can disclose if we have a little dab or a big dab of larceny. (Grade yourself) Do we take ❏ hotel towels, ❏ paper clips, ❏ pencils, ❏ candy, ❏ clothes, ❏ money, ❏ jewelry, ❏ newspapers? Add your own ❏ _____ ❏ _____ ❏ _____.

Kousin Zeke sez, "If we does anyone of these we deserve jail. Now don't squabble with me. Fuss with Moses and Jesus, 'cause they wrote the RULE BOOK." So what can we do? If needed and it's possible, Make amends. Ask God for forgiveness. If we steal, take or borrow, STOP. What will be the results? Peace of mind sleep, sleep like a baby. For some it may keep us out of jail. Believe me THAT'S A HAPPY THOUGHT.

A footnote: A store manager said, "Like it or not somebody's paying for all the stealing somewhere. It's YOU and ME."

MISSING SOME BRICKS

A talk show host told this for a true story. A man who was a bit slow, decided to rob a bank. He went in and wrote a note on the banks deposit slip. This is a Stick up, give me some money. The man stood in line and began to worry that possibly someone saw him write the note. So he decided to go to the bank across the street. He gave the same note to the teller at this bank. The teller, a smart girl, noted as she read the note with it's bad spelling, that this man was missing some bricks. So she said, "Sir, our bank can't accept notes written on another banks deposit slip. You will have to take your note back to the other bank." The man did, he went back to the other bank. The teller called the police and the man was arrested.

You say, "That man is really missing some bricks." What about some of our dumb decisions? Let me tell you about some people who were just as dumb. A TV star who confessed on national TV, "I knew better but now I'm HIV." An employee decided to borrow, steal that is, from his company. His bonus was prison time instead of vacation time. Some teens had a choice, coke or beer, the beer won out, they were killed with their buddies. A friend of mine, a dog lover, lost everything, his business, wife and children over dogs. His dogs were at the DOG TRACK.

Kousin Zeke sez, "Them folks is missing some smarts, 'cause they could have asked the Good Lord for COMMON SENSE and saved themselves heaps of troubles. Does it ever cross your mind, why some folks, maybe some of us, ain't been in jail? AIN'T BEEN CAUGHT YET."

℞ FIND BURIED TREASURES

I was driving my car in Tampa, Florida when a car passed me with a bumper sticker that caught my fancy. The sticker read, Ask Me About Buried Treasures. Curiosity got the best of me, so I followed the car to the next light, stopped my car next to his, rolled down my window and asked, "What's with the treasures?" All the time my mind was conjuring up some idiotic advertising gimmick. The man said, "Don't you know? The treasures are found in the Bible".

Kousin Zeke sez, "When my mind gets all cluttered up and I don't know which end is up, I read the advice of King Solomon. He 'vises to have 'Two goals, wisdom-that is KNOWING and DOING RIGHT and COMMON SENSE'. The person who knows right from wrong and uses good judgment is happier than the person who is immensely rich. My Jesus tells me, 'Don't store up treasures here on earth where they can erode away or be stolen. Store them in heaven where they will never lose their value.' That is some good 'vice if we have 'nought sense to heed it."

Appears to me, Kousin Zeke and King Solomon know where the authentic treasures are to be found. Be thankful they are NOT BURIED and are AVAILABLE for EVERYONE, just for the ASKING and USING.

DUMB EXCUSES

A pastor was visiting with a church member who had been absent from church worship for some time. She began to tell him about all her fun activities. She explained, I have been fishing, golfing almost daily and playing soccer and tennis with the kids." The pastor commented, "I don't believe I've seen you in church lately." She replied, "Pastor you're right, I haven't been able to attend because I have a bad leg." IS THAT A DUMB EXCUSE OR NOT?

Do you ever attend a church or a religious service? Why or why not? Kousin Zeke sez, "I don't know 'bout you but me and my family needs to spend time with our Lord. When we misses worship our family is like a bunch of sore tail cats in a house, fussing and acting upright nasty to each other. Even worser, we are just plain ornery with other people. I know one thing, I shor misses my Lord 'cause I needs him more than he needs me. When I'm asked, 'How come you ain't been in church worship lately?' I can thinks up more DUMB EXCUSES THAN YOU CAN SHAKE A STICK AT."

Always remember, the church is for down-and-outers, sinners, hypocrites and whosoever and guess what, for you and me? What can we learn from the lady with the bad leg? Never allow any person, situation or some DUMB EXCUSES to interfere with our personal relationship with our Lord. Make churchgoing a habit. It can only hurt good.

BEST BEAT SPOUSES

Did you ever hear of a BEST BEAT Dad or Mom? Probably not. I know you've heard of DEADBEAT Dads and Moms. Anyway, BEST BEAT Dads and Moms are those who love each other and care for their children through thick or thin. Their marriage is punctuated with stick-togetherness and no cheap, selfish bail-out. Most DEADBEAT Dads and Moms slam-dunk their spouses, do their own thing, marry again or find a live-in, eat, drink and try to make merry. Then complain because they have to pay child support and accept responsibilities for their own children left behind. Meanwhile the discarded spouse has to make a valiant attempt to survive and their children must suffer the consequences.

Kousin Zeke sez, "When DEADBEAT Dads and Moms desert their spouses with little regard for the welfare of their children, they is knocking on the door of hell itself." You say, "Zeke that's a strong statement." Zeke sez, "You think so, then read what Jesus sez, 'If any of you causes one of these little ones who trusts in Me to lose their faith, it would be better for you to have a rock tied to your neck and be thrown into the sea." The way I read it, if we are guilty we better be making some amends and NOW." Let's make a 110% effort to share caring love to all children and our spouses. Let's all be BEST BEAT Dads, Moms and Friends. This will put smiles on our faces and FOR CERTAIN in the hearts of children.

℞ ENCOURAGEMENT

Some encouraging words for you and me in a poem written by a wounded Confederate soldier. One source says that this son of South Carolina was wounded during Picket's charge at the Battle of Gettysburg. No one knows where he was when he wrote these words. Maybe lying on a Pennsylvania battle field in the hot July sun, or perhaps he was in a hospital recuperating from battle wounds. But wherever you are at this moment, the words penned by this soldier will speak encouragement to your heart:

I asked God for strength, that I might achieve,
    I was made weak that I might learn humbly to obey,
I asked for health, that I might do greater things,
    I was given infirmity, that I might do better things,
I asked for riches, that I might be happy,
    I was given poverty, that I might be wise,
I asked for power, that I might have the praise of men,
    I was given weakness, that I might feel the need of God,
I asked for all things, that I might enjoy life,
    I was given life, that I might enjoy all things,
I got nothing that I asked for–but everything I had hoped for,
    Almost despite myself, my unspoken prayers are answered.
I am among all men and women richly blessed————copied

Uncle Peter sez, "For heavens sake, read this poem over and over til we learn what this soldier said bout prayer."

℞ TEN SUGGESTIONS

Most people can quote a few of the Ten Commandments. Quoting them does not necessarily indicate that we understand what they mean. The meaning of the Ten Commandments is not too difficult to comprehend, if we are honest with ourselves and are willing to straighten up and fly right. That's the problem for many people because to them the Commandments are only Ten Suggestions and they can do their own thing, usually it's to eat, drink and make merry.

A cartoon in a magazine, Christianity Today, shows Moses on Mount Sinai holding the Ten Commandments. Moses is looking toward heaven and he is saying to God, "The people tend to lose interest rather quickly. Could I have some one-liners instead?" You could say God did that 'cause even a ten-year-old can explain their meaning.

1. Love the only true God.
2. Don't make an image of God.
3. Honor His Name.
4. Keep His day holy.
5. Honor your parents.
6. Don't murder.
7. Don't commit adultery
8. Don't steal.
9. Don't lie.
10. Don't covet.

A lawyer friend of mine, John Strauss, told me, "Jack, it's strange but in the Tampa courthouse there are volumes and volumes of books explaining all the laws. But all the laws can be summed up by the Ten Commandments. God gave the laws in love and for the good of mankind and that includes you and me."

WHY THE FOURTH OF JULY?

A large airliner touches down and comes to a halt on a runway at a major airport. In just a moment, a group of Marines come out of the airplane and remove four flag-draped caskets. With precision movements they put the caskets on foundations. They backed off and stood at attention. These four Marines had died for you and me. This same scene has been duplicated thousands of times.

Thousands of women and men fill veterans hospitals all over America. Many are blind, crippled and totally ignored by many of us. What's your feelings of the MEMORIAL and FOURTH of JULY holidays? For millions it's time off from work, school, picnics and have FUN, FUN and FUN.

JULY 4th marks the birth of a new nation conceived in liberty as a product of our Christian faith and dedicated to the proposition that all people have an inherent right to LIBERTY, JUSTICE, and EQUALITY of OPPORTUNITY.

As we celebrate MEMORIAL and FOURTH of JULY HOLIDAYS, let us remember those who have paid the SUPREME PRICE FOR OUR FREEDOM. Don't forget to remind yourself and others in the midst of their FUN, FUN, what is the REAL PURPOSE of the HOLIDAYS. It was not fun for those who SACRIFICED FOR OUR FREEDOMS. Remember to THANK GOD and REJOICE that we can celebrate. THEY CANNOT.

℞ THE BOTTLE HABIT

"Bottle habit can be easy to break." This was the title to an article in The Tampa Tribune. The writer was asking parents to write in and tell her how to get a 2-year old off the bottle without severely upsetting the child. The chief of behavioral pediatrics at one hospital said the answer is shockingly simple. He listed some steps parents can take. But how do you get 13-75 year old's off the bottle that began with social drinking and is disrupting themselves, families and jobs?

Most people who have an alcohol problem won't believe what I'm saying - one major hospital, that treats persons with drug problems regularly announces on TV "If depression and alcohol is ruining your life, call us for help. If you don't get help here, please get help somewhere."

BELIEVE IT OR NOT, anyone can become a problem drinker or an alcoholic by social drinking. It all begins with the first drink. Alcohol is a drug. Beer is especially dangerous because most people consider it harmless. SAD TO SAY, many who believe this will end up in the HOSPITAL, JAIL, OR FUNERAL HOME. The worst part they frequently take the innocent with them.

There is a simple answer, like the doctor said about a 2 - YEAR OLD BOTTLE PROBLEM. If you drink, JUST SAY NO. Kousin Zeke sez, "Don't be no BOTTLE BABY, be FULL GROWN. When you does this, ASK THE GOOD LORD FOR HELP, THANK HIM, THEN HELP OTHER BOTTLE BABIES."

℞ FIXING THIS GOOFED-UP WORLD

I was thinking one day, what's one problem with this crazy mixed-up world? So I decided to ask Kousin Zeke, he has dabs of common sense. I found him sitting on a barrel in a country store. This is what he told me, "One of the worser problems it 'pears to me, loose sex is spreading like rag weed. This ain't nothing new, a disciple wrote about this over 2,000 years ago, just like he knowed 'bout TV,"

"The people claimed to be wise without God. They became fools, instead. God let them go ahead into every sort of sex sin and whatever they wanted – yes vile and sinful things with each other's bodies. Their lives became full of every wickedness. They were fully aware of God's judgment, yet they went ahead and did them and encouraged others to do them." Them words even make ol' Zeke do some thinking.

Does it ever cross your mind what's the SOLUTION for FIXING UP THIS GOOFED-UP world and how to know RIGHT from WRONG? Bobby Bowdoin, the outstanding coach of the Florida State football team, told in his book, 'More Than a Game', how to know right from wrong. Bobby said, "I hear folks moan when I say, if you don't know what God wants, then you haven't read the Bible. Read the dad-gum book! God will tell you what to do. He will shape your life."

Zeke sez, "That's shor am some dad-gum good advice to heed. I am, 'cause on judging day, I have to give an account. I struggles to obey them just like you. If you have to complain, talk to Moses and Jesus, they made the rules. If we obey what they say, PEACE and HAPPINESS shor do come easier."

SANTA – A SYMBOL

Do you believe in Santa Claus? What's your opinion of Santa Claus? Do you believe in miracles? One movie that is shown every Christmas on TV, is Miracle on 34th Street. The theme of the movie is easy to understand. Is Santa Claus for real or a fake. In the movie, Santa did everything he was supposed to do, he loved children, spread joy and encouraged generosity but the business people became greedy and attempted to mar his image for selfish reasons. Santa was taken to court and before a judge. Santa Claus represents what's right in the world, love, joy, peace, forgiveness and unselfishness. These values are the opposite of hate and greed.

Santa is a symbol of the positive values that create a better world, communities and families. So what if you see scrooges', skin-flints, nerds and the lack of goodwill in this world, don't let this bug you, just be the kind of person you ought to be. Kousin Zeke sez, "I ain't never seen so much giving and love as I see at Christmas time. Uncle Peter ain't spoke to me in 20 years, yet he gives me a pair of socks and pays me back money for a cow he stole. All I knows is Santa represents what the world, me and my family needs and why God let his son be born. And I ain't so stupid as to debate bout Santa, I just gives the Good Lord a big thanks and sez what can I do to make this a gooder world. Let s do it together."

THREE BERRIES

But officer, I only had three berries. Yes, but you and your flying buddies crashed into buildings. You were flying so recklessly that some of your friends were injured and some killed. You say, "But Jack I don't get it. How can a few berries create such havoc?" This was the newspaper article in Iowa City, Iowa. DOZENS OF MIGRATING SONG BIRDS STOPPED OFF FOR REFRESHMENTS AT A DOWNTOWN BERRY TREE and ended up grounded for DRUNKEN FLYING. This time of the year berries were beginning to ferment. The birds were eating wine. Fifty of the birds flew into windows and a handful died. "The bar is closed for the night" said the Animal Control Officer. When she arrived at the scene, roughly 30 tipsy birds clung to the tree branches, another 40 were passed out around the trunk.

Have you ever read after a tragic auto accident, a domestic quarrel or an embarrassing, stupid decision? "Hey, I only had about three (berries) beers. I can control my drinking. Yeah, just like the birds." Kousin Zeke sez, "I ain't seen nobody and I mean nobody that can control wine, beer or alcohol. If you doubts me, read or watch the daily news. Let's do away with the doubts. How? Don t eat no more fermented berries and you will have PRESCRIPTIONS FOR HAPPINESS galore."

℞ DON'T MISS THE BASICS

Does it ever pass through your mind? Is this world UP-SIDE DOWN or DOWN-SIDE UP? Everyone is asking this question. Kousin Zeke sez, "It shor do 'pear to me, most people giving out advice on how to be UP-RIGHT in this DOWN-SIDE world, have no earthly idea how to do it, 'pears like the institutions have released their inmates who are now in charge".

One solution that keeps popping up, RETURN TO THE BASICS. Here are some people that are trying to RETURN TO THE BASICS. Army secretary, T. West said, "As a means to correct our problems, we will return to the basics, which are traditional American values." A headline read, "A Push to teach Ethics and ABC's." Who made that statement? The American Association of School Administrators. They said, "Ethics should permeate the entire school process." A women's golf magazine had as a video title, "Return to Basics." The first chapter in the instruction manual for Microsoft Windows 95 is 'The Basics.' Vince Lombardi the renowned football coach, after his team had played a poor game would hold up a football and say to his team, "This is a football and the basics for winning are blocking and tackling."

Jesus didn't have a computer or even E-Mail but he did have B-Mail (Bible Mail) and that's where we can learn about the BASICS of daily living. We can MISS lot's of this world's JUNK and TRASH but for heaven's sake don't miss the REAL BASICS. For a start, do what this short TV blip said, "Think of doing something good for someone else."

BETTER THAN THE AVERAGE BEAR

Do you want to do better than a bear? Yogi Bear says he is better than the average bear. Do you want to be better than average? Some don t give a hoot. Do you know what a SYNONYM is? It is a word having the same meaning as another word. If you're satisfied with being average, this will shock you. Why? Some SYNONYMS for average are: TOLERABLE, MEDIOCRE, COMMONPLACE and RUN-OF-THE MILL. Kousin Zeke sez, "If you is stranded in one of these categories, you is like a swimmer in a raging river floating gleefully down stream, with no desire for swimming up stream."

I knew a lady that did not believe in social drinking. She was fearful of what others would think. When she attended a party she walked around with an empty glass in her hand as though she were drinking. This is what you call peer pressure. When we lose the battle to peer pressure, we become average and this is doom time or going along with the crowd. Even Jesus had some followers like this, when he needed them they were hanging out with the wrong crowd.

How can we conquer AVERAGE, MEDIOCRITY? You don't have to be a genius, just DO YOUR BEST, GIVE YOUR BEST. As Kousin Zeke would tell you, "Give life your best shot, call on the Good Lord and man there is no way you can be average. You might even be like Yogi Bear, be BETTER THAN THE AVERAGE BEAR.

JUST DON'T DO IT

The FLU BUG is bad and I mean bad. I had the bona fide flu once. I didn't die but I wouldn't have argued about dying.

There is another BUG running rampant, especially in stadiums. Kousin Zeke sez, "This bug is worser than the FLU BUG." It's called the BOO BUG. The BOO BUG ATTACKS SPORTS TEAMS, COACHES, PLAYERS, OFFICIALS and FANS. The BOO BUG can be transmitted just by sitting next to someone who has the BUG. A father can easily give the BOO BUG to his children. The BOO BUG is really a hate bug but you say, "I don't hate when I boo. It's sorta fun." I say ill-mannered fun. Where does "Do unto others" fit in with booers?

Kousin Zeke sez, "You can get shots for the FLU BUG but there ain't none for the BOO BUG. The best medicine for the BOO BUG is a DOSE OF COMMON SENSE DECENCY and the best and only cure is DON'T BOO. I hopes and prays you never catch the FLU BUG and especially the BOO BUG.

WHAT IS IT WE DON'T DO?

DON'T BOO!

(NOW THAT IS A PRESCRIPTION FOR HAPPINESS.)

℞ GRAINS OF SAND

If you owned a Corvette sports car you would want only the best care for your car and what is the best oil to use. Major oil dealers will give you lots of advice. Their ads say this. Add New Life to your Engine - Works Like Liquid Ball Bearings - Protects In Ways You Can't - Best For Fuel Economy. Man, that's some good advice. Suppose someone comes along and tells you, "Use our product. It's the best and will make your engine run smoother and provide peace of mind driving." You say, "That's for me, I'll use your oil." Then the man replies, "Oh, I forgot to tell you, we've added a special additive. We include two or three grains of sand in each quart of oil." You reply, "Only a fool would put grains of sand in a cars' engine oil." Yep, you're correct only a fool would but every day millions of people are doing exactly the same thing. How's that?

People possess the most SOPHISTICATED, COMPLEX, INTRICATE machine ever created, it's their BODY. The grains of sand are BEER, ALCOHOL AND OTHER DRUGS. Beer is especially destructive because most people consider beer harmless. Many people believe they can drink socially and grains of sand will not harm their bodies (engines). Don't Be Fooled.

Ask individuals in every walk of life who have lost jobs, families, fortunes and lives, not forgetting the untold stockpile of sorrows and heartaches. There is a SIMPLE SOLUTION. If you honestly desire to stop putting grains of sand into your engine (body), JUST DON'T. If you're offered grains of sand, JUST SAY NO, I AIN'T NO FOOL, I loves' my body and my car. Now that's a one healthy prescription for good living.

BOOSTER SHOTS

The comic strip, Garfield, shows Jon telling Garfield, I'm depressed Garfield. After I'm gone no one will care that I ever existed Garfield said, Hey cheer up Jon - They don't care now. Does it ever cross your mind, that possibly no one in this cotton picken world gives a hoot whether you live or die.? Lots of folks have that notion and sad as it is, many have a valid reason for believing that no one cares. Recently I was paying for my meal at a restaurant. The young girl at the register was very attractive and had a beautiful smile. I remarked that she had a WINSOME SMILE and was a BIG PLUS for the restaurant. She replied, "Thank you for your very nice compliment, I REALLY NEEDED THAT BOOST TODAY."

I said to my wife, "That girl certainly needed a BOOSTER SHOT TODAY, TO BUOY UP HER DEJECTED SPIRIT." Matter of fact, she could have used a DOUBLE DOSE OF JOY PILLS. I believe her lack of joy was not really her fault. Why? She was probably passed by lots of well-meaning, busy and even some caring people but they were consumed by ME, MINE and OURS. They failed to comprehend that she just needed a DAB OF ENCOURAGEMENT.

Every day you and I mingle with lots of folks like Garfield's friend and the girl at the cash register. Folks need BOOSTER SHOTS with TENDER LOVING CARE. How can we give these shots? Kousin Zeke sez, "It ain't no big deal. Every morning before your bare feet hit the cold bedroom floor, DECIDE to be a PAL, be PRAYERFUL, AVAILABLE and LOVING. The Good Lord will place WHOSOEVERS in our path who need His love. How? Remember, it ain't no big deal, JUST PASS ON DABS OF ENCOURAGEMENT.

℞ THE BEST IN THE WORLD

How does a person qualify to be acclaimed the best in the world in his profession? That's the reputation of one man determined by his peers. How could a person be judged so highly? Is it because he eats hot-dogs or wears pretty ties? Not really, he is in a profession that requires skill and mucho practice. He's a golfer.

The golfer's name is Jack Nicklaus. Here is the primary reason he is considered to be the best in the world. It's explained in a statement he wrote on the back cover of a book, "PLAY BETTER GOLF. I'VE TRIED ALL MY LIFE TO GIVE EVERY SHOT I HIT, IN PRACTICE OR IN PLAY 100 PER CENT EFFORT."

Kousin Zeke sez, "I'm like lots of folks cause I don't understand why a person would take a stick and knock a ball far as he can and then go chase it, but people does."

What about you and me? Do we usually give our best or do we complain 'cause life ain't give us nothing? I'm not suggesting everyone take up golf but I'm saying we give 100 per cent in all we do. Kousin Zeke sez, "If you runs to win and gives 100 per cent you may not be the best in the world but you will be the best with your family and those who knows you. Even the good Lord might put a star in your crown and that ain't bad." Kousin Zeke is right on, because the Apostle Paul said, IN A RACE, EVERYONE RUNS TO WIN. SO RUN YOUR RACE TO WIN.

ARE YOU A WINNER OR LOSER?

Are you a winner or loser? What makes a winner? Imagine you are playing in a tournament and your team ends up in last place. Are you a winner or loser? I was visiting in a home with a father and son. The father said to his son, "Jimmy, go get your trophy and show it to Jack. He's a sports enthusiast and will appreciate seeing your trophy." The 12 year old son brought the trophy into the room, with a dejected look and joyless voice said, "We did not win, we lost, this is a second place trophy." I asked him, "Did you play and give your best?" Jimmy said, "Yes sir." I said, "Guess what? You didn't lose you won." The scoreboard may indicate a point lost but it's in our hearts that we win in sports and even in the GAME OF LIFE.

The sports world is totally obsessed with winning and being NUMBER ONE. Most fans cannot accept losing. The fans say, "We don't care what you did last year, give us a winner now." The attitude to win at any cost is prevalent in little leagues, big leagues and every phase of sports.

Kousin Zeke sez, "Ask yourself, Am I an authentic winner or just another poor loser. If you are on a team that comes in first, second or last and you gives and plays your best you are a winner. NEVER FORGET, there is another scorekeeper, he's the one I wants to please 'cause he keeps the score, knows the rules and rewards the winners." Be a REAL WINNER and be HAPPY.

℞ WHAT NUMBER TO CALL

A distraught mother came to our front door, screaming at the top of her voice, My baby has stopped breathing, please help me. I began CPR while 911 was being called. In a few minutes the police and rescue squad arrived. Thank God the baby did begin to breathe on its own. Who do you call when facing a crisis? Often I thank police officers and rescue teams for what they do. Why? They are usually only a phone call away. In most parts of the world there is no 911 to call and often no phone.

You may say, "Jack, I'm thankful for the protection of 911 but who can I call when my heart is breaking and I'm at my wits end?" Guess what? Kousin Zeke sez, "It ain't no big deal, you calls Psalm 91, if you don't knows, it's in the Bible." The next time you've been knocked down by life and need solace for your heart, read Psalm 91. Here are a few words of comfort from it.

"God is my refuge and place of safety. Don't be afraid of the dark any more, nor fear the dangers of the day. He orders his angels to protect you. They will steady you and keep you from stumbling. He will give you a full life through his son." Kousin Zeke sez, "When my heart or body is spilling, over with hurts, I calls on the One I need. I thank God for both, cause you can t go wrong with either number. One favor you can do a friend or even a stranger, tells them about the other 911 number, Psalm 91.

HOW TO MAKE A DIFFERENCE

Do you ever wonder why you are in this cotton picken world? Do you ever imagine, is there anyway you could make a difference, for good, in this world? David Wolpe told this story in Readers Digest. A man once stood before God, his heart was breaking from the pain, prejudice and injustice in this world. "Dear God," he cried out, "Look at all the suffering, the anguish and distress in your world. Why don't you send help?"

God responded, "I did send help. I sent you." When we begin to wonder what we can do to repair and sew up the seams of this broken world, the answer is not too complicated. JUST REMEMBER, God sent his son, Jesus, this is the authentic message of CHRISTMAS. He also sent you and me to be a blessing and to share the blessings of CHRISTMAS with others not just not just for an instant or a year but for a lifetime. Kousin Zeke sez, "Giving out blessings to others is what makes life fit fer living, fer me and even for my dog, ZEB."

℞ FOUR LETTERS - TGIF

Let me tell you about four letters and they do not spell a four letter word. The four letters do make millions of people extremely happy for a brief period of time. I heard a DJ, radio disc jockey, shout with enthusiasm, "THANK GOD FOR TGIF." This is a phrase voiced by employees who are bored, tired and cannot wait until CLOSING TIME ON FRIDAY. Why, they're looking forward to a week-end of eat, drink and make merry. What do the four letters signify? "THANK GOD IT'S FRIDAY."

I really can't knock this attitude since often I think the same thoughts about Friday's. But sad to say, this same DJ who had hopes of a fantastic week-end, SOMEHOW LOST THE GLITTER WHEN MONDAY ROLLED AROUND. The DJ said in a mournful voice, "What's the cure for MMB, MONDAY MORNING BLUES." I guess he forgot, MONDAY'S STILL FOLLOW SUNDAY'S.

I don't know what daily tribulations you face but I can assure you, almost without exception, there are others as Kousin Zeke would say, "Much, much worser off than you is." If you permit it, life will KNOCK you down, KICK and SPIT on you. But LOOK UP, THANK GOD and COUNT YOUR MANY BLESSINGS. There is a song that reads, COUNT YOUR BLESSINGS and NAME THEM ONE BY ONE. When daily life has overwhelmed us, let's do what the song says, PAUSE FOR A MOMENT, BEGIN COUNTING OUR BLESSINGS. Then we can thank God for EVERY DAY of the WEEK and not just TGIF.

℞ BAND-AIDS NEEDED

Why in this up-side-down or down-side-up world would a cartoonist draw a picture of this world with a Band-Aid around it? The title he wrote at the bottom of the cartoon explains why. "A HURTING WORLD." This is a hurting world for millions of people. The words to two country songs sorta gives us an insight into the hurts and frustrations of lots of folks. "You Are Wanted By the Police and Your Wife Thinks You Are DEAD" and "Take This Job and Shove It, I Ain't Working Here No More." There is another song that explains about an ointment that can help remove Band-Aids from this world and from you and me. The song title, "What The World Needs Now Is Love."

The sad part millions of folks never encounter the genuine love of God or love from others. Why? Most of us are so involved with "me," "mine," and "ours" that we fail to understand the heartaches and loneliness of others, and often will not take the time to understand. Kousin Zek sez, "And even worser, we sidetracks loads and loads of joy and happiness when we do not take time to share concern for others. Me and my family have been doubly blessed by others who have had bad times like us, and by the good Lord who is always available. What we gonna do now? 'Cause we've been doubly blessed, we gonna do our dead level best to help remove Band-Aids from others."

Kousin Zeke has given us a good prescription. Let's commit ourselves to do likewise. (Share this article with others.)

FOOTPRINTS

One night a man had a dream. He dreamed he was walking along a beach with the Lord. Across the sky flashed scenes from his life. For each scene, he had noticed two sets of footprints in the sand, one belonged to him, and the other to the Lord.

When the last scene of his life flashed before him, he looked at the footprints in the sand, he noticed that many times along the path of his life there was only one set of footprints. He also notice that it happened at the very saddest times in his life.

This really bothered him and he questioned the Lord about it. "Lord, you said that once I decided to follow you, you'd walk with me all the way. But I have noticed that during the most troublesome times in my life, there is only one set of footprints. I don't understand why when I needed you most you would leave me."

The Lord replied, "My precious, precious child, I love you and would never leave you. During your times of trial and suffering, when you see only one set of footprints, it was then that I carried you."

Author Unknown

* * * * *

Without question, this is one of the most widely read and printed inspirational articles in recent years. It is found on greeting cards, pictures, bulletins and even bed spreads. You will hear it read at club meetings, churches, schools, funerals and even at political and AA meetings. Why? FOOTPRINTS expresses the heartfelt hunger and need of everyone for carrying their daily cares and worries.

If you have a heartache at the moment, ask Him to carry it for you. He will.

℞ A GOOD NIGHT'S SLEEP IS POSSIBLE

WHEN WAS THE LAST TIME YOU HAD A GOOD NIGHT'S SLEEP? This was an ad in a Tampa newspaper by a hospital s Sleep Disorders Center. The ad continued, If you have trouble getting a good night's sleep, you're not alone. Sleeplessness has become a common problem for millions of men and women. Not only can it lead to fatigue and reduce alertness, it can harm your health." We don't need a college degree to understand that our lack of sleep can cause us to be stressed out. There is a tried and proven prescription. It does not require a pill or drug. It is the words of a 1911 hymn. If we sincerely make these words our prayer, we can clean out any cobwebs or sins in our lives. Make this a daily habit and it can provide comfort, peace of mind and allow us to sleep like a baby. (These words are also printed in "Happy Thoughts To Keep and Give Away".)

An Evening Prayer[1]

If I have wounded any soul today, If I have caused one foot to go astray,
If I have walked in my own willful way, Dear Lord, forgive!

If I have uttered idle words in vain, If I turned aside want or pain,
Lest I myself shall suffer thru the strain, Dear Lord, forgive!

If I have been perverse, or hard or cold, If I have longed for shelter in Thy fold,
When Thou hast given me a fort to hold, Dear Lord, forgive………

℞ WHO CAN WE BELIEVE?

WHO CAN WE BELIEVE? Does that thought ever run through your mind? It should, since we are blitzed daily with lies. If you doubt it, read some of the ads that are pitched at us a gillion times every day: NONE BETTER, NUMBER ONE SELLING CAR, NO STRONGER PAIN RELIEVER, THE WORLD'S BEST, NO CREDIT or BAD CREDIT. One of the best TV programs is Andy Griffith. The program always has a moral lesson to teach its viewers, but in one episode Andy goofed-up. He was trying to sell an antique cannon to a stranger, and he stretched the truth. Standing nearby was his son, Opie and his deputy, Barney. Andy did such a hard sell that ol' Barney offered to buy the cannon. Andy convinced the stranger to buy the rusty cannon. That evening at home, Opie showed Andy a new pair of skates he had just bought. Andy was shocked and said, "Opie where in the world did you get the money to buy new skates?" Opie replied, "Dad, I just talked like you did today. I traded an old worn out glove for skates, I copied you." Opie's remarks put a guilt trip on Andy, and he had to confess that he goofed-up big time. He then asked Opie to forgive him for setting such a rotten example.

We live in a hard sell world, and we must make a choice. Are we going to allow the world to shape and forge our values? Kousin Zeke sez, "Now this ain't a happy thought, but according to the good book, all liars will get a vacation in Helena, and it ain't in Helena, Montana. The good news is, we can be forgiven if we sincerely ask God for forgiveness. " Never forget, IF WE ALWAYS TELL THE TRUTH WE WILL ALWAYS KNOW HOW TO ANSWER.

GET A DAB

Do you possess COMMON SENSE? Do you know what it is? Would you use it, if you had it? Kousin Zeke sez, We have to decide what matters and what don't. If our priorities is all screwed up, it's time to ask the good Lord for a big dab of COMMON SENSE and enough sense to use COMMON SENSE." Let me tell you about two men who had enough sense to use their sense. The owner of a worldwide hotel chain, was asked, "What is the one thing you wish every customer in one of your hotels would do?" He replied, "When they take a shower, put the shower curtain inside the shower." C.S. Lewis, a world renowned author, theologian and lecturer was asked by a student, "If I come to Europe, what's the most important thing to bring?" C. S. Lewis answered, "Bring warm underwear." You may say, "Why Jack, those are two stupid answers?" No, they did not respond with the answers most of us would expect or give but they did give COMMON SENSE answers.

Here's what one of the wisest men of all time, King Solomon, said about COMMON SENSE several thousand years ago. "Have two goals, (1) WISDOM, that is, knowing and doing right, and (2) COMMON SENSE. Don't let them slip away." Solomon also said, "The person who knows right from wrong, and has good judgment and COMMON SENSE is happier than the person who is immensely rich." Don t let these two goals pass us by. That's Godly advice.

A DUMB FROG

I read a story about a frog. The frog was wondering how he could get away from the cold winter climate. Some wild geese suggested that he migrate with them. The problem, though, was that he couldn't fly. "Just leave it to me," said the frog. "I've got a clever brain." He thought about it and then asked two geese to help him by picking up a strong reed, each holding one end. The frog planned to hold on to the reed with his mouth.

In due time the frog and geese started on their journey. Soon they were passing over a small town, and the villagers came out to see the unusual sight. Someone cried out, "Who could have come up with such a smart idea?" This made the frog so puffed up with a sense of importance that he exclaimed, "I did it!" His pride was his undoing, the moment he opened his mouth he lost his hold on the reed and fell to his death.

Where does FALSE PRIDE rear its ugly head: IN SPORTS, "How come I don't get to play more? I'm a much better player. I'm gonna take my ball and go home." IN THE WORKPLACE, "I've worked here longer, but 'ol' Joe was promoted. He's the bosses favorite." IN CHURCH, "They never let me sing a solo. I never get thanked." IN SCHOOL, "I should have gotten a better grade, but the teacher dislikes me."

It's not difficult to be PUFFED UP and PROUD, if we caress and love ourselves and permit our minds to DWELL ON ME AND MINE. Kousin Zeke sez, "On the other hand, just to enjoy a smudge of happiness, all that's required is to love others like we love ourselves. Then, be careful what spills out of our mouths."

That ain't big deal unless we're proud and selfish like the frog.

℞ KNOW WHO IS CALLING

Did you read about a so-called dumb sheep that prevented his shepherd from going to jail? The story is told of a man in Australia that was arrested and charged with stealing a sheep. But he claimed emphatically that it was one of his own sheep that had been missing for many days. When the case went to court, the judge was puzzled, not knowing how to settle the matter. At last he asked that the sheep be brought into the courtroom. Then he ordered the other man who claimed he owned the sheep to step outside the courtroom and call the animal. The sheep made no response except to raise its head and look frightened. The judge then instructed the defendant to go outside the courtroom and call the sheep. Then the accused man began to make his distinctive call and the sheep bounded toward the door. It was obvious the sheep recognized the familiar voice of his master. "His sheep knows him," said the judge, "Case dismissed!"

One of the most meaningful pieces of literature ever written and perhaps the most read is the 23rd Psalm. It has been read over and over again for thousands of years by millions of people. It's all about a shepherd and his sheep. The 23rd Psalm in reality is a prescription for abundant living, which will help us live a healthy and balanced life. Living in the complexes of life's pressures and conflicts, one fact is certain, everyone needs the uplift promised by listening to the shepherd's voice. Kousin Zeke sez, "If I wuz you, I would read the 23rd Psalm over and over 'til I could recognize the shepherd's voice when he calls." Lots of voices are calling, but we need to hear the voice of the authentic Shepherd who offers peace in times of stress and turmoil. Be certain you have answered HIS CALL.

℞

Jack, how come no words?

Hey Jack, you goofed up. You left all the words off this page, it's blank, why? Most people are like me, too much blabbing and too little listening. We're so busy spouting off about ourselves we fail to hear what others have to say. The good book gives some super advice, "If you have ears, listen." If you want a happy heart, be a good listener. How? Listen to others. A good start, listen to shut-ins or go to a nursing home. OK, I hear you, I ain't gonna write one more word.

℞ BE SPICY NICE

Would you like to FEEL, THINK and BE young? Most of us can. Hey, Jack do you mean we can drink from the fountain of youth? Nope, and I m not talking about being young and foolish, but to be young at heart and happy. Let me tell you about "SPICY." SPICY was her given name. In her daily living she demonstrated the meaning of the word Spicy. She faced trials as everyone does, but she always remained young in spirit. She never dwelled on bad news or the past. A clean joke, laugh or funny story was always available to be shared. If you promised SPICY the moon, she still would never reveal her age. Why? SPICY was young in spirit. She was SPICY NICE.

Jack, how do you know so much about the lady named SPICY? Because SPICY was my mother and she survived 24 hours a day rearing four Kelley boys and grand children. She lived by faith on the happy, spicy side of life and not on doom street in gloom city.

Kousin Zeke sez, "Do you live in gloom city and want to move out? If so, let me tell you how to move out: (a) Don't listen to, watch or read the daily bad news, (b) Don't live in the past, live one day, better yet, live one second at a time." 2,000 years ago Paul told us how to think, "Fix your thoughts on what is true, good and right. Think about things that are pure and lovely, and dwell on the good things in others. Think about all you can praise God for, and put into practice all you have learned." If we half-way follow this advice, we will think YOUNG and live on HAPPY street in JOY city. The answer is clear-cut, just be SPICY NICE.

℞ INGS CAN DO US IN

Do you ever have a problem with INGS? Most of us do and it ain't easy to win out over them. Fact is, many people never win the battle. The INGS destroy lives, families and send lots of folks to the divorce court, jail, hospital and often to the funeral home. Some who don't make it to the funeral home, almost wishes they had. Jack, what are you trying to tell us? "Just read on."

Here are some of the "INGS" that can DO US IN and I mean do us in Bad. Lying, Hating, Stealing, Gossiping, Cheating, Drugging, Drinking, Sexing, Worrying and Griping. If one of these ain't your bugaboo, think of one that is. If you can't think of one, ask a friend to tell you. All of us are confronted with some type of temptation, unless we're dead. Is it possible to win the battle with "INGS"? I'm not saying it's a piece of cake, but we can. A desire of 99.9% sounds good but to be a winner an effort of 110% is required. The truth is best understood by a cartoon showing two boys discussing the matter of temptation. One boy said, "What you need to do is to resist." The other boy replied, "I would but it may never come again."

Kousin Zeke tells us how to conquer the "INGS." " (a) Decide we wants to, this is a must, (b) Do what the good book sez, (c) Keep forgiveness up-to-date, (d) Just do what we know is right. Do not check our E-Mail or computer, check our heart, then we will HAVE A HAPPY HEART and so will lots of folks.

I JUST TOOK A PENCIL

Did you ever hear that laughter is the best medicine? It can be a very good medicine. Readers Digest carries a section called, Laughter, The Best Medicine. They tell this story. It seems Peter was manning the Pearly Gates at heaven's door when 40 people from New York City showed up. Never having seen anyone from the Big Apple at heaven's door, St. Peter said he would have to check with God. God instructed him to admit the ten most virtuous from the group. A short time later, St. Peter returned breathless and said, "They're gone!" "What" said God. "All of them are gone?" "No" replied St. Peter. "I'm talking about the Pearly Gates, they stole them." You say, Jack nobody could do that. You're right, that's stupid, but not any more idiotic than two boys robbing some ladies selling Girl Scout cookies.

Did you hear about the man who complained about the big white FLUFFY towels in hotels? He said, "They're so big I can't get them into my suitcase." That's supposed to be a joke but it ain't no joke for hotel owners. Stealing is a financial disaster for everyone, 'cause somebody has to pay for all the thievery. Guess who? It's the customers, you and me.

Uncle Peter sez, "I thinks 'bout as much of a thief as I do a liar. They both will do 'bout anything else, if they gets the chance. If we steal a pencil, stamp or a thousand dollars do we deserve jail, yep? Stealing ain't nothing to laugh 'bout 'cause one of these days we are all gonna stand before the Good Lord and gives account. I wants to hear, Peter you done good, come on in. Now that will place a dab of laughter in our hearts."

TRY COURTESY

What's the answer to this riddle? (Something you can see and you can't see. Can hear and you can't hear. Can keep or give away?) Give up? It's COURTESY. Is winning at all costs the most important thing in sports and in life or should athletes and fans try to win with good manners? This was the question posed to a star-studded panel of athletes, coaches and officials. They debated the role of sportsmanship with today's athletes and fans for 90 minutes on prime time national TV. Why? Because the decline of sportsmanship, worldwide, is so appalling. One sports fan was asked, "Do you spell courtesy with a "K" or a "C"? He replied, "I don't know, I never use the word." Believe me, courtesy is the missing ingredient in much of our society today. If you doubt it, read the papers or watch TV. The actions of some fans were described as maniacal.

It is usually the few maniacs or fringe lunatics who create much of the chaos, yet their bad behavior is often mimicked by much of the crowd. There are jerks in every aspect of life, but we cannot permit them to derail our positive actions. Kousin Zeke sez, "We don t throw in the towel, we just keeps on keeping on. Lunatics are like the seven year itch they just keep on itching. What can we do? The answer ain't complicated, Just Treat Others Like We Want to Be Treated."

LIVID RAGE IN 10 SECONDS

I got myself roundly cussed out the other night. It happened after I opened a door onto a sidewalk, narrowly missing a woman who was walking there with a little boy. Without breaking her stride the woman told me to watch where I was going. I begged her pardon. She began yelling the kind of language I can't repeat. Half a block away she was still cussing me out. This was part of an editorial by Leonard Pitts, a columnist for the Miami Herald. He said, "I kept replaying it in my mind, wondering how the woman had gone from a minor annoyance to a livid rage in 10 seconds. Maybe you've been there. Someone cuts in front of you or snatches your parking space. Suddenly, you're dodging shrapnel and wondering why."

What's the remedy? It ain't no piece of cake but we must not permit the fringe lunatic or looney to make us respond in the same maniacal behavior. Life is too short. I've made up my mind, I'm not going to let any person or situation make me live in fear or on doom and gloom street, at least not for long. Make up your mind to do likewise.

Ol' Kousin Zeke has a common sense prescription on how to win out, "(1) Be a shining light in a darkened world. (2) Be bigger than they are (Whoever they is), (3) Keep prayed up and ask the good Lord for all the faith he can spare, (4) Make this a daily habit, give away POLITENESS, KINDNESS and LOVE to others, whether they respond in love or hate. That's what me and my wife calls living high on the hog. Try it YOU WILL like it."

NEVER A LOSER UNLESS YOU QUIT

Some remarks you WILL NOT HEAR often, if ever at sporting events, Coach if I don t get to play that s OK with me. I don t have to be on the starting team. If you take me out of the game I will understand and will not be upset. Some remarks you DO HEAR at sporting events, Coach, I expect to be on the starting team. If they take me out of the game, I promise you, I won't be happy. If I don't get more playing time, I'll probably quit the team. I think the coaches have favorites. You say Jack, "Those players are acting like children or babies." That's right, Kousin Zeke sez, "They don't need a ball they needs a bottle." The missing fundamental is TEAMWORK, playing as a unit and not as individuals.

The coach of a championship football team said, It's true; we don't have the quality players as some teams but we play together as a team. Marcus Allen received the award as the best running back in the NFL. On national TV, he explained in detail about his teammates who made it possible for him to win the award by their blocking and making holes for him to run through.

It's funny but not so funny, TEAMWORK is necessary for happiness with individuals, families and anyone living on this planet. While I was writing this article an announcer on TV introduced a girl's basketball team that had only won one game that year. In their last game they only scored two points while their opponent scored more than one hundred points. The announcer asked one girl, on the loosing team "How do you do it?" She replied, "You are never a loser unless you quit?" Today we have too many losers because they quit. Let's decide to play as a team and be a winner. And you know what? Lots of folks will be winners.

℞ GOSSIP AIN'T NO GAME

Here s a game you may wish to try at a party. Get the people to form a circle, then tell a story and ask each person to whisper the story to the person next to them. Make up a story similar to this one. Jack and Jill went up a hill to get a pail of vinegar, coming back down they brought two goats and three bales of hay. God only knows what the last person would be told. I can assure you of one fact, it would not relate to the original story. Jack, what are you trying to say? This is exactly how GOSSIP BEGINS. I asked you to play a game but in real life GOSSIP ain't no game. GOSSIP destroys reputations, families and lives. Too often the results are worse than deadly. I have more respect for an alley cat than for a GOSSIPER.

Large headlines in the Tampa Tribune read, "John Doe EXAGGERATED, lawyer says." The lawyer should have said, "My client lied." Evidently some people are convinced there ain't no harm if we fib and exaggerate. Exaggeration is not the truth! Many people pass it off as, "I need to make a point," but more often it results in character assassination.

Kousin Zeke sez, "If I could get one request from the Lord, I would ask that GOSSIP have an odor like alcohol or a skunk, believe me, that would shut up much of the idle blabbing." Remember, what goes 'round comes 'round. When we blab with loose tongues, these blabbers will blab about us. What's the ANTIDOTE? (1) Ask God to forgive us, (2) If needed make it right with someone we have wronged, (3) Don't GOSSIP, (4) Make this a life time habit: IF YOU CAN'T SAY SOMETHING GOOD ABOUT OTHERS SAY NOTHING.

℞ THE DEVIL'S BEATITUDES

Blessed are those who are too tired or busy to
worship in church each week.
They are on my team.
Blessed are those who enjoy criticizing and judging
the choir, clergy and other church members.
Their hearts are not in it.
Blessed are those who wait to be asked and always
expect to be thanked.
I can use them.
Blessed are those who are touchy and grouchy.
With a bit of luck they will stop attending.
They are my missionaries.
Blessed are those who claim to love God at the same
time are hating other people.
They are mine forever, my kind of people.
Blessed are the troublemakers.
They will be called my children.
Blessed are those who have no time to pray or to give.
They are easy prey for me.
Blessed are you when you read this and think it is about
other people and not about yourself.
I'VE GOT YOU.

(Unknown-copied and adapted)

RIGHT NOW!

Recently I saw one of the most unusual posters I have ever seen. It was a solid black poster, and in the center of the poster were only two words, "RIGHT NOW." I wondered what nut thought up the idea for this poster, and what was the poster trying to say. I soon learned. There was another black poster behind the first poster, with three words in the center. Can you even guess what the three words were? When I read the three words, I realized the words were conceived in the mind of a genius. Remember, the first poster read, RIGHT NOW. The words on the second poster read "NOT NEXT WEEK." The world could almost be transformed over night , if most of us stopped our dilly dallying and procrastinating.

I read a poem, entitled, "THE STRENGTH OF ONE." (author unknown). I've changed the title to, "BE THE ONE." This poem helps to explain the meaning of the posters.

One smile can start a friendship - One handclasp can lift a soul –

One bird can make you sing - One candle can erase the darkness –

One laugh can chase the gloom - One vote can change a nation –

One prayer can reach Jesus - One sunbeam can light a room –

One step can begin a journey - One star can guide a ship at sea –

One hope can raise our spirits - One prayer can show you care –

One person can make a difference.

Do you ever wish you could put a Band-Aid on this hurting world? You can, BE THE ONE to make a difference, RIGHT NOW and NOT NEXT WEEK.

I LOVE MY?

I Love My Dog - I Love My Parakeet - I Love My Beer - I Love Shopping - I Love Golf. Here are a few of the bumper stickers you often see on cars. Some are funny, some are cute, some are crude and many are ridiculous. What is your number one love, or the one thing you love more than anything else on this planet? I asked Kousin Zeke what was his number one love. He didn't tell me, but he did tell me this story, "It seems a man wanted to know how to get to heaven, so he asked the Lord, 'What do you have to do to get to heaven?' This was the answer he received, 'You know what the Commandments say - don't commit adultery, don't murder, don't steal, don't lie, honor your parents, and so on.' The man replied, 'Oh! That ain't no big deal, I've obeyed all those since I was a child.' This really was a lie since no one can keep them all. The Lord made a statement which really blew his mind. He said, 'There is one thing you lack, sell all you have, and give the money to the poor.' When the man heard this, he was dumbfounded. He sadly walked away, for he was very rich. I presume his bumper sticker would read, I Still Love My Dollar Bill."

I asked Kousin Zeke, "Where did you read that story?" He said, "I read it in the good book and it shor has kept me, my wife and kids on the happy side of life. We do know what s the fitting message to place on our bumper sticker, cause the right sticker will produce bushels of joy and happiness."

INSIDE OR OUT

What would you think if you were an artist and you painted a picture over seven feet tall and four and one half feet wide? The picture became so famous it was shown in exhibitions all over the world. John Ruskin said, "I believe there are few people on whom the picture will not produce a deep impression." The picture was shown in Australia, and one writer said, "Australia is seethed with crackpots and predators of unwary souls." Most of the crackpots said, "Few people will come to view this picture." But the people came by the thousands.

World renowned artist, Holman Hunt, was born on April 2, 1827. He painted three versions of the picture between 1851 and 1900. Today the picture is still touching lives.

After the world tour, the picture was placed in one of the most famous cathedrals in the world, Saint Paul's Cathedral in London. Each year it is viewed by thousands.

The title of the picture is "The Light of the World." The picture shows Christ standing in front of a vine covered door and knocking on the door. Once, another artist was looking at the picture with Mr. Hunt and said, "Mr. Hunt you have painted a masterpiece, but you have made one mistake." He replied, "What's that?" The man said, "You left the door handle off." Mr. Hunt responded, "That's not a mistake, I purposely left the handle off. I want everyone to know that the door handle is on the inside. Christ stands knocking at everyone's heart, and since the door handle is on the inside, only we can open the door." I am trying to paint the message of Revelation 3:20, Look I am standing at the door of your heart, if you will open the door, I will come in and offer you peace and guidance. A thoughtful question, is he on the INSIDE or OUTSIDE of our hearts?

JOE'S TOWN

I heard an unusual story about a man who decided to move to another town. He visited many towns. In one town he stopped in front of a country store, where two men were sitting on a bench. He got out of his car and asked the men a question. "Have you lived here all your life?" The men said, "Yep." Let me ask you another question, "What kind of town is this? Is it a good place to live and rear your family?" One of the men was named Joe. Joe said, "Let me ask you a question? What were the people like where you lived?" He said, "They are loving, generous and very helpful." Joe responded, "Sir, You would enjoy living in this town." The next day the two men were sitting on the store bench, when another man drove up. This man was also quizzical about the town. He said to the men, "Gentlemen, I'm interested in moving to this town, and would like to ask you some questions." Joe, said "OK, what do you want to know?" The man said, "Is this a good town to rear your family, are the people considerate and honest?" Joe replied, "Sir, let me ask you a question. What were the people like where you used to live?" He paused and then said, "They are greedy, self-serving and just a bunch of hypocrites." Joe responded, "Friend, you would never want to live in this town, you would be miserable here." The man left.

Joe's friend said, "Joe, why in the world did you encourage the man not to move here?" Joe responded, "This man was hateful and greedy and saw this in all his townspeople, if he moved, he would bring his own baggage of selfishness. What about us, would Joe invite us to live in his town? That s a good question to ponder.

JUST BEING POLITE

Let me ask you a question? Is being polite more than saying "please" and "thank you"? Suzanne Chazin said it is, in an article for Readers Digest, "How to Raise Polite Kids in a Rude World." I agree with her 100%, yet with a "but" later. "Miss Manners" columnist, Judith Martin, certainly makes a similar statement. "Being courteous is more than simply saying, 'please' or 'thank you,' it's not boasting (bragging) or calling someone names behind their back, its about winning fairly, losing graciously, and treating others with respect." Kousin Zeke sez, "some of the so-called championship teams, players and fans should let what Miss Manners said, sink into their inflated, cocky and egotistical heads. What's they need is, just a dab of humility, but because of their swell-headedness I guess there ain't enough space left. This ain't true just in sports, it's true in everyday activities. If you doubt it, listen 'round, we might be surprised what spills out of our mouth, or maybe what don't spill out. Do we make a habit of saying 'please' and 'thank you' or 'yes sir' or 'yes mam' at home, work or play? I will 'til they puts me in under."

According to an etiquette expert, "Manners aren't about using the right fork. Manners are about being kind, giving compliments, team-playing and making sacrifices. Children learn this through their parents and adults." Remember, I said at the beginning of this article, that I agreed with Suzanne Chazin 100% that being polite is more than saying "please" and "thank you." What's my "but?" But, even if you don't use the two phrases, begin today. You will be happily flabbergasted at the results, even your dog may come back home. You could get a raise, for certain you won't get fired. Your family and friends will like you better. If you have doubts, ask them.

NO BINOCULARS ON THE TITANIC

Imagine yourself on the Titanic. The ship is traveling at 21 knots an hour, into an ice zone, littered with floating ice and icebergs, some over 100 ft. tall. The ships officers had already been warned about the dangers of icebergs in the area, and were asked to be watchful. The lookout sitting in the crows nest was not so watchful. When he came on duty, he had misplaced his binoculars and said, "I don't really need them, because I can see just as well without binoculars." His intentions were good, but his eyesight failed him. While on watch the Titanic plowed into an iceberg, and you know the rest of the story.

A reporter wrote, "Anyone with just a dab of common sense, should not be on watch duty without binoculars." Everyday millions of people drive past highway billboards, that warn about icebergs, and never give them a second thought. Somehow our eyesight is so poor the messages never sink in. Possibly some of us are a bit near-sighted.

If you have doubts? Read these: (DRINK-DRIVE-DIE), (GAMBLING IS ADDICTIVE), (KIDS, DON'T START SMOKING), (WIN LOTTO-LIVE LIKE A KING).

Kousin Zeke sez, "If our eyes and brains ain't working together, we best make an appointment with an optometrist (eye) doctor. My optometrist is the Good Lord. He has a 911 number, and his office is open 24 hours daily. He don't care if we is yellow, black, white, poor, rich, smart, dumb, famous or a nobody. If our eyesight is bad or even poor, take the eye exam in the good book. You will be happily surprised how much your vision improves."

PEEP IN THE BOX

The story is told about a bereaved wife sitting in a country church at the funeral service for her husband. She was sitting with her small son, Jimmy. The gentleman giving the eulogy waxed strong with exaggerated praises. He mentioned how generous her husband had been with his family, how he loved his wife, and his faithfulness to friends. The speaker continued with his magnified platitudes and almost compared her husband to a sainted angel. After about thirty minutes listening to this man, the shocked and dumbfounded wife whispered to her son, "Jimmy, go up there and peek into that box, and see if that is your Pappy, I believe the funeral director put the wrong man in the box. They're talking 'bout a man I ain't never knowed."

We all have been in similar situations. I'm not opposed to passing out compliments. Fact is, most people would achieve a "F-" for failing to give thanks and praises to others. What's the point, Jack? Always tell the truth and be honest. There are two facts that can put a smile into the hearts and lives of others.

If you can't say something good about others, then DON'T SAY ANYTHING.

If you can say something good about others, then SAY IT TODAY, NOW – TOMORROW may be too late. Can you think of someone that could use a compliment or a kind word from you? A SUPERFINE habit to cultivate, GIVE FLOWERS TO THE LIVING.

℞ HAPPY HABITS

Do you ever wonder why some people are HAPPY and cheerful while others are UNHAPPY and miserable? Do you ever feel like you lost your last friend, or that nobody in this cotton picken world cares whether you're dead or alive? Maybe you've been wishing and praying for just a smudge of happiness. There are some happy habits, if we just take the time to make them a part of our daily living that can put a touch of joy in our lives.

1. Think First of Someone Else
2. Be Kind, Be Gentle, Give a Soft Answer
3. Laugh and Smile
4. Express Your Gratitude
5. Apologize When You are Wrong
6. Seek Out a Forgotten Friend
7. Write a Loving or Thank you letter
8. Be a Good listener
9. Help Others
10. Visit Sick and Shut-ins
11. Forgive and Forget
12. Pray Often
13. Attend Church Regularly
14. Share Your Faith
15. Live Love, Live It Again, Live It Still Again.

Kousin Zeke sez, "To have a happy heart, be certain you have faith in my Lord. Practice some of these HAPPY HABITS each day, then your BLUES WILL BURST INTO SMILES."

Adapted from a church bulletin

WWJD

Do you know what the letters WWJD mean? If not, I will explain them to you later. A man arrived late for a meeting, as soon as he went in he said I don t know what you've said or done, but I'm against it. This is the same remark a spoiled kid makes when he is substituted in a ball game, "If I don't get to play more, I'm going to take my bat and go home." Often disgruntled employees say, "So and So is the boss' favorite, that's why I didn't get advanced." Or, "This marriage will work if you do things my way."

This negative attitude is encountered in all of life, businesses, schools, sports, families and churches. It's sad, often in churches, members want everything done their way, if not they pout. A lady told my wife, "I go to church to worship God. I keep my eyes on Him and not other people. In this manner, I always discover the best in others, and guess what? I always have peace of mind." A lady asked Billy Graham, "Dr. Graham, can you tell me where to find a perfect church?" He replied, "No I can't, but if you ever find one, the minute you join it, it will become imperfect, because you are imperfect."

A big fad with many youth today, is to wear four letters on bracelets, T-shirts, etc. The four letters are WWJD. If we have a problem in our home, school or business, I would suggest we copy the youth and ask ourselves WHAT WOULD JESUS DO? Following this example could solve most of life's problems. For one thing, it can only do good. Kousin Zeke asks, "How does that grab you? It can only grab us good, 'specially if we are willing to do what's right."

DON'T ASK ME

Do you like to be around miserable people? I don't. Let me tell you about a man I don't want to be around and I mean never, NEVER SPELLED WITH CAPITAL LETTERS. I passed this man as he entered a store. He had on a T-shirt with this message printed on the front of his shirt. The letters were very large in bright colors, "I AM RETIRED, DON'T ASK ME TO DO ONE D— THING." People with this attitude live dismal lives. They are usually arrogant, touchy and hateful. For them it is usually too hot or too cold, too wet or too dry, too early or too late, too much or too little. Many are like the man who complained that his wife cooked the wrong egg. They are angry most of the time, and spend their waking hours fault finding. They just need to get a life.

Kousin Zeke sez, "What these people needs is a kick in the seat of their pants 33 times a day. They really do need the kicks, but don't kick them, just do right, as difficult as it is: **Love them anyway, Pray for them and for patience, Be a good example, Let their garbage go in one ear and out the other**. When possible, remind them what Paul told us to think about over 2000 years ago, 'Fix your thoughts on what is true, good and right. Think about things that are pure and lovely, and think on the fine and good things in others. Think about all you can praise God for, and God's peace will be with you." Let's pray one for another that our patience can endure, 'cause when our patience departs us, we gotta remember the one we can call on, The Good Lord.

KIDS TALK

Did you ever learn anything in Kindergarten? Steve Fulghum wrote, All I Really Need to Know I Learned in Kindergarten. I learned how to live and what to do. I learned to share. Play fair. Don't hit people. Put things where you found them. Clean up your own mess. Don't take things that aren't yours. Say you are sorry when you hurt somebody. Wash your hands before you eat. Live a balanced life. Learn some and think some. Take a nap every afternoon. Watch out for traffic. Hold hands and stick together. Goldfish and hamsters all die, so do we. Everything you need to know is in there somewhere. The golden rule, love and sanitation. Ecology, politics, equality and sane living. Think what a better world it would be if we all, the whole world had cookies and milk about three o'clock every afternoon. If all governments had a basic policy to always put things back where they found them and to clean up their own mess."

This article about the kindergarten explains plain 'ol' common sense living in kindergartner language. Translated into adult terminology (words) it is saying: love others, play together as a team, don't be a show-off, forgive and forget, keep filth out of your mind, love and serve the Lord, do unto others, don't hate, lie or steal and clean up your own goof-ups. We don't need four degrees to understand what this article is saying. One fact is certain, if we want to change the world for better, just do what we learned in kindergarten. If this kindergarten talk is too fancy to understand just ask any kindergartner to explain it to you.

I AIN'T ADDICTED

Do you have an addiction? Addictions can be good or bad. Let me tell you abut the lady who had a basketball addiction. She lived in a state that had two colleges with competitive basketball teams. The lady was sitting at a sold-out championship game with an empty seat? A curious fan came up and asked, "Why isn't someone sitting in that empty seat?" She replied, "Oh that's my husband's seat, and the rest of the family have gone to his funeral." That's a funny story, but let me mention some addictions that ain't so funny.

(Alcohol) Beer and Wine - (Gambling) Lotto and Casinos - (Stealing) Whatever and Whenever - (Lying) About Anything - (Hating) Anyone - (Gossiping) You Name It - (Profanity) Trash Mouth - (Abuse) Need Jail Time - (Internet) Good and Bad. The Tampa Tribune had this headline, "Pitfalls Await Unwary on Internet." Parents need to know about the dark alleys of cyberspace where pornographers, hate-mongers and child-molesters dwell. This warning is for everyone.

Kousin Zeke sez, "If we really want to quit our addictions, when everything is said and done, the solution is up to us. We can't blame nobody else. To quit, there are some steps we must take. (a) Decide we don't want to do it no more. (b) Do the opposite. (c) Get help if needed, go to a support group and a church. (d) Pray something like this, "Dear Lord Jesus, I need help, I'm helpless. I ain't playing a game this time. Forgive my goof-ups (sins). Thank you for listening to my puny words, Amen." If we halfway do these steps, I promise you and me will be happier, and so will LOTS and LOTS and LOTS of FOLKS.

DON'T LET YOUR 4th BE A 5th

Will your 4th of July be a 5th or even a 6th of July? If it's a 5th (fifth of whiskey that is), there will be a superfluity of drinking, if it's a 6th, there will be a multiplicity of six-packs. Oh, there will be lots of playing and much fun-time. When the eating begins, everyone will dive in, never once looking up. Like pigs, most will jump in, start swallowing their food and never offer even a thanks.

If your 4th is a genuine 4th of July, it's true there will be lots of drinking, not fifths or six-packs, but soft drinks, even some root beer. There will be loads of playing and fun-time. The food will be scrumptious and more than filling. If it's a patriotic 4th of July celebration, before or after the people eat, there will be a shared moment of gratitude for all their blessings. Those present will dive in to eat, but not like pigs, they will look up and thank God for freedom.

Together, let's pledge to make this and every 4th of July, a time of gratitude for those who have sacrificed so much, in order that we can live in a free land with peace and happiness. Also, commit ourselves to never, never permit our 4th of July to become a 5th of July.

JUST MISS IT

Will you be here when the Apocalypse occurs? What is the Apocalypse? The Tampa Tribune had this headline explaining the Apocalypse. APOCALYPSE - WOW. A five part documentary takes a harrowing look at ways the world might come to an end. Walt Belcher, a Tribune writer, wrote, "Will the world end in a puff of smoke or a ball of fire? Will humans be wiped out by a killer virus, a nuclear blast, global warming or a wayward asteroid? Take your pick, Apocalyptic scenarios abound." As we approach or pass the year 2000, millions of people are asking when and how will the world end?"

Interest in the end of the world is at a fever pitch because of the stressful time in which we live, says an English professor at the University of South Florida. One Tampa TV station aired these specials, - Ends of the earth - Doomsday Asteroid - Natures Fury – Nuclear Holocaust - Killer Virus - and Climactic Catastrophe. Just thinking about the consequences of these titles could put us in stress town, awake with nightmares. Even a ton of sleeping pills wouldn't help.

Webster's Dictionary defined Apocalypse in Jewish and Christian prophecy, the ultimate destruction of Evil (Satan) and triumph of Good (God), found in the last book of the Bible, Revelation. The reality has been secularized by human-caused threats and Hollywood.

Kousin Zeke 'plains his view, "I believes all this stuff 'bout the Apocalypse, 'cause it's in the good book, and we're all in the game of life. The Good Lord invites us to join his team. Me and my family joined his team, 'cause he ain't lost a game, and we want to go to his Super Bowl." You can too, just tell him something like this, "Lord, I ain't much of a player, and I ain't on no team. I need a coach and would like to play on your team. You know what he would say? Hey that puts you on my team, you can begin playing now, and you will miss the Apocalypse.

SQUASH THE BUGS

I read about planting a different garden in a devotional. Kemmons Wilson, founder of an international motel chain quoted some advice for planting a "garden" that would enhance our work skills:

- Five rows of "peas" - prayer, preparedness, promptness, perseverance, politeness.

- Three rows of "squash" - squash gossip, criticism, and indifference.

- Five rows of "lettuce" - let us love one another, let us be faithful, let us be truthful.

- Three rows of "turnips" - turn up for church, worship, turn up with a new idea, turn up with the determination to do a better job today than you did yesterday.

That is some good advice about our work skills but also about our living skills. I don't know what kind of garden we are planting for ourselves, our family and others. If our garden ain't doing too good, maybe we need to do some replanting and add a load of fertilizer. Then spread insecticides to SQUASH THE BUGS…that's destroying our children, homes, and families. Believe me. A healthy garden will produce fruits of love, joy and peace in a home, a family or a nation. Kousin Zeke sez, To learn how to grow good fruit, read Galatians 5:22 in the good book.

IS GOD BLACK OR WHITE?

I read an article that asked the question What color is God? If you want to sound like an idiot, try to answer some questions from kids. That's the question James McBride, an African-American author, asked his Jewish mother when he was a boy. His autobiography contains the following story. Walking home from church one day, he asked her "Is God black or white?" His mother said, "God is not black. God is not white. God is the color of water. Water does not have a color."

The writer of the article said, "That was a wise response. We know God does not have a color because he is a spirit. He is present everywhere we are. Whether we're sitting at home or flying miles above the earth. He is there and we can call out to him. He is always open to our cry. He isn't an idol or an idea. God is a spirit, ever available."

Some people say they do not believe in God. When I was in the Navy, I remember when planes were bombing our ship, a young man told me afterwards, "I was literally frightened to death, in those seconds I saw everything I had done wrong in my life." When people say, they don't believe, don't believe it. Just wait until they hear the "C-word" by a doctor, or a tragedy happens to them or to someone they love. As the saying goes, "There ain't no atheist in foxholes." I read about the atheist that was engaged in a public debate about the existence of God. To emphasize a point he was making, the atheist wrote these words on a blackboard: "God is nowhere." In rebuttal the Christian simply split the last word so that the statement read, "God is now here."

God's color is not important, but that He is ever available to give comfort and assurance is!

℞ DEPRESSION

A man asked his doctor, Why am I depressed? The doctor replied, If you don't stop worrying so much, your depression will kill you. The man said, "Doc, that's the most depressing thing I've ever heard." Depression ain't no fun thing, but we do not have to live under a cloud of anxiety and depression. If we watch, listen to or read the bad news daily, we will have a nervous breakdown every 15 minutes. A one-half page ad in a Tampa newspaper asked, "Does You Life Have Signs of Persistent Anxiety? Have you been worried by unrealistic worry?" The ad showed six boxes with these words in each box: IRRITABILITY, MUSCLE TENSION, RESTLESSNESS, DIFFICULTY CONCENTRATING, FATIGUED, SLEEP DISTURBANCE. The ad said, "If you are affected by three of these see your doctor." I don't know anyone that's not affected by some of these at one time or another, I am. The ad was promoting a non-habit forming pill. I do not know of any pill that's not habit forming. A friend told me he was addicted to Alka Seltzer.

Kousin Zeke sez, "I ain't no doctor, but I can give you a prescription that can cure depression or anxiety:

1. Laugh at life.
2. Forget the past, it ain't coming back.
3. Stop doing your thing, do the Lord's thing.
4. If you need to forgive someone, do it today.
5. Realize pills, alcohol and drugs ain't no cure.
6. Read and do what the Good Book sez.
7. Find someone hurting, help their hurt.
8. Visit the Lord's house regularly, then you'll be happier and so will everybody else.

GOOD OR GOODER

When you get good, do you get gooder? When you get to be the best, do you get bester? For many people in life and sports this seems to be the trend. One golfer had a phenomenal winning record for a short period. He began to boast how great he was, and compared himself to one of the greatest golfers of all time. He turned out to be just another golfer. One NFL football team had a team loaded with first round picks. The majority of players were judged to be the best. They began the season by winning most of their games, headed for the Super Bowl. The problem, the super players began to super squabble with each other. **Pride** and **Jealousy** raised its head. Not only did the team not go the Super Bowl, they did not even win their division title.

In the business and sports world it is not unusual to hear, "We're the biggest and the best." If you don't believe it, ask them. There is nothing wrong with having self-confidence, but their attitude goes far beyond playing as a team, it becomes I'm number one. You can like it or lump it.

There is a ladies college basketball team that has won three straight national championships. Last season they won every game, and were acclaimed by many as the best ladies team ever. They have the nation's best player, plus an all-star team returning. You have to wonder, will pride and egos be the stumbling blocks for this team. Let's hope this talented team will play together as a team, be their best in sportsmanship. If they do, the team will be a champion. This principle applies to every aspect of daily living. If we play and do our best we will always be champions, win or lose.

JUST FOR FUN

It will never happen to me. So what if I play the lottery, bet on a game, play a slot machine in Las Vegas, gamble on a cruise ship, in a casino or at bingo. I don't care what you say. I will never become addicted to gambling. I just play for fun. Most people that gamble will not believe what I am about to write. America is in the midst of a cancerous gambling epidemic. If you doubt this, read what my friend Karl had to say about his gambling habit.

"I argued and reasoned with my family and friends, that gambling is just a fun thing. Let me tell you, it turned out to be anything but a fun thing. I gambled for over thirty years. I took my family and kids through Hades. I lost two homes and one family. I never imagined that gambling would turn me into a liar, a thief and a no-good bum. I never owned a gun, because I knew my wife would shoot me." His wife told me this was absolutely true.

Somewhere in the midst of Karl's frightening battle with gambling, the Lord touched his life. A few years ago in Tampa, Karl began a Gamblers Anonymous in a church library. Only eight people were present, but because of this first GA meeting, today there are Gamblers Anonymous meetings all over Florida. If you wish to know about the heartaches as a result of Gambling, just ask some family members of Gambling addicts. You say, Jack is it that bad? It must be or there would not be highway billboard signs on I-75 reading, "Gambling is Addictive. Call this number for help." A poem in the Gamblers Anonymous handbook explains what helped to change the life of Karl and others. "I sought my soul, But could not see, I sought my God, But he eluded me, I sought my brother, and found all three." If you need help, do as Karl did, say "Lord I need you.

℞ WITS-END

How many times have you said, I am at my wits-end? What can I do with my worry and fears? How can I stop worrying? I can t recommend a pill, but I can give you a prescription that works. I once heard of a man who walked along a road, tired, weary and discouraged. He could hardly put one foot ahead of the other. A neighbor overtook him in a wagon and invited him to ride in the wagon. As they started down the road, his neighbor noticed that the weary man still carried a heavy sack of grain on his back. "Put the sack down," he said, "You don't need to carry that." The tired man said, "Oh it's enough for you to carry me, let alone this sack of grain." There are thousands of people like this man. They have turned to God, but still are carrying their burdens, when God begs of them, "Give me all your cares, for I care about you."

How sad it is that our WORRYING continues in one vicious circle. What can we do? Jesus said, "Don't let your heart be troubled." The word "let" indicates we do have control over our WORRYING. Kousin Zeke sez, "The Lord knows our hurts and gave us a prescription for our hurts. This ain't no new prescription, it is found in Proverbs, the third chapter, the fifth and sixth verse. These verses explain how to cure WORRY IN THREE DOSES." 1. TRUST your worry to God (without reservation). 2. Do not MEDDLE. Let God work it out in His own time and manner. (You then can win out over your worst enemy, your thinking.) 3. DO GOD'S WILL regardless. (Put God first in every area of your life). God's promise to us after following His prescription in verse six, "I can help you handle any situation, if you will trust and obey me." Take and use this prescription as needed. God s office is open 24 hours daily.

CLOCK STRIKES 13 TIMES

Did you hear about the man whose clock went haywire and struck 13 times? The man said, It's later than I ever knowed it to be. If you are like me, you think like this man. The world is going haywire, I must be the only human being on this earth, especially if you try to use a phone. It sounds like this, "Do you have a touch-tone phone, if so push 1, if not push 2, if you like this option, push 3, if a collect call push 4, after tone, leave a message on voice mail. Goodbye."

Recently I was in another state and needed to call back to Florida for an emergency. I tried for fifteen minutes to get my call through, I never did. The automatic operator reminded me repeatedly that their company was adding new equipment, for better, quicker and cheaper service. I never once spoke to a living, human-being. I wondered, "Am I the only person left on this earth?"

The attitude of much of society appears to be, just be bigger and faster, forget courtesy and being people-persons, just get the job done. One of the largest and most successful financial institutions in Florida will not permit their personnel to place incoming calls on hold, refer their customers to another operator, or listen to elevator music. This company has learned how to make friends and increase business. The words of a country song sum up the attitude of many people today, "Honey, if no one calls, that's me."

Uncle Peter sez, "It don't take no mathematician to figger out, when we lose plain 'ol' politeness, we lose it all." Little courtesies take little time but can brighten lives. What can you and me do? If someone is rude be nice, if mean be sweet, if hateful be loving.

DO YOU HAVE HS?

Do you have HS? Do you know what HS is? My wife and I have it. Sad to say, we've had it most of our lives and didn't recognize it. HS can create tons of headaches and even heartaches, not only for those who have it but for those we give it to. Someone asked, "Is HS a disease?" Not only is it a disease, it's an uncontrollable epidemic.

How did I learn about HS? I heard one psychologist discussing HS with another psychologist. They did not call it HS. They called it Hurry Sickness, because one of the psychologists had written a book called "Hurry Sickness." The book discusses the problem for those of us who are living in this hurry-scurry world. Too often, HS affects our attitude and we become rude, hateful and just plain ol' mean-tempered. This disease attacks us at the most inopportune times, in traffic, when shopping, at the airport, at restaurants or the post office. One sad note, HS creates chaos in the home and often violence and bodily harm results.

Is there a cure for Hurry Sickness? First, we must realize we have a problem with hurrying through life. Second, decide we want to slow down and smell the roses. Next, find some slow down habits and practice them. Someone suggested a good safety habit for traffic. I recommend it highly. When waiting impatiently at a red light, and the light turns green, count three before moving forward. I've tried this four times. I would practice it more, but I don't have time. It is a good prescription for staying alive. There is even a better one, "Love is patient and kind, never haughty, selfish or rude." I would like to write more about HS, but I have to make two phone calls, write a letter, visit a friend, and be at the airport in two hours. Oh! I gotta go, I hear my wife calling.

GRADE YOURSELF

Would you grade yourself, happy or miserable, how bout halfway happy or halfway miserable? Let me share a thought with you. Most of us blame our miseries and problems on our circumstances. If things don't go to suit us, we immediately blame someone or something. Here's a fact, we should file in the depths of our minds forever. This truth can help us survive the very worst of circumstances, and weather life's storms. **"We cannot choose our circumstances, but we can change our attitude toward them."**

I read about Dr. Viktol Frankl, who was imprisoned at Auschwitz, where he was stripped of his identity as a medical doctor and forced to work as a common laborer. His father, mother, brother and wife died in the concentration camps. All his notes, which represented his life's work were destroyed. Yet Dr. Frankl emerged from Auschwitz believing that everything can be taken from a man but one thing: the last of human freedoms – to choose one's attitude in any given set of circumstances. If we live on this planet, the time will come when some circumstance will knock us down, then tromp right over us with a smile.

Read how ol' Uncle Peter handles the detestable side of life, "I practices what the disciple Paul said, 'I have learned not to gripe or grumble, regardless what kind of mess I'm in.' It ain't easy, and sometimes it's a chore to do, but peace of mind and heart is my reward." Remember, WE CANNOT CHANGE OUR CIRCUMSTANCES BUT WE CAN CHANGE OUR ATTITUDE.

℞ HYPOCRITES

Here is an astonishing fact. When we point our index finger at someone or something, three of our fingers are pointing directly back at us. If you doubt this, point your finger at someone and look at your hand. Yep, three fingers are pointing back at us. Jack, what are you trying to say? Too often when we spread rumors, plain ol'' gossip or repeat what so and so told us we are more guilty than they. A first-class check-up, look at the direction of our three fingers. We might be embarrassed, if guilty we are…specially if we practice judging habits, gossiping that is?

The best treatment and cure for the judging disease is explained by Jesus to a bunch of self-righteous hypocrites. As he was speaking to a crowd, these so-called friends, brought a lady to him and said, "She was caught in the act of adultery, and she should be punished. What about it?" They continued to demand an answer. Jesus stooped down and wrote in the dust with his finger. He then stood up and said, "All right throw the first stones, but only he who has never sinned may throw the first stone." The so-called friends slipped off one by one, leaving only Jesus with the lady in front of the crowd. He said to her, "Where are your accusers? Didn't even one of them condemn you?" "No sir," she said. He said, "Neither do I. Go and sin no more."

If the truth of this story speaks to you, as it does to me, take this TEST before judging anyone: First: IS IT TRUE? Second: IS IT NEEDED? Third: IS IT KIND? If we fail this test keep our mouths shut. Kousin Zeke sez, "The good book sez, if someone stumbles, we should lovingly help them back on the right road, and share each others problems. That ain't bad, only good."

℞ BE A PLUS AND NOT A MINUS

Do you ever think, the sports fans in this world have gone completely berserk? I do. In today's paper the headline read, Umpire shover gets jail term. The judge said, The public is fed up with poor sportsmanship." If you need more convincing, read this article which was in the Tampa Tribune, "Cheers and Jeers." The Jeers won. Two college bands playing at halftime, brawled for twenty minutes, sending three members to the hospital. For me, this one wins the booby prize.

If you are a sports fan, you probably want your team to be number one in all sporting events. Let me suggest one area that any team can be ranked as number one. It's better than winning the national, conference or division championships. How is that possible? Be number one in SPORTSMANSHIP and COURTESY. One major university, The University of Tennessee, encourages anyone associated with the school to practice courtesy and sportsmanship. What are they doing? Before each football game begins, for over 100,000 fans, their band plays a salute to the visiting fans and team. Before the game begins, for over an hour, six signs inside the stadium, alternate playing these messages: "FOOTBALL FANS ARE REMINDED TO OBSERVE THE SPIRIT OF GOOD SPORTMANSHIP AT TODAYS GAME — REMEMBER UT's REPUTATION FOR FRIENDLINESS TOWARD OUR VISITORS." Joan Cronan, the ladies athletic director, makes sportsmanship and courtesy her number one priority. You say, doesn't this school still have nerds and jerks? Sad to say they do, but they are trying to overcome the bad effects of the poor sports, by encouraging sportsmanship. Thank God, they realize there is a problem in sports, so they are trying to be a plus instead of a minus. Let us copy their example.

PRESCRIPTION FOR HAPPINESS

Will Rogers said, I never met a man I didn't like. But I never met a man or woman that didn't want to be happy. The sad part, too many of us do not realize there are some prescriptions for happiness. A man gave a prescription over 2,000 years ago. He described some of the garbage that can steal our joy. He wrote, "Stop lying, just tell the truth. If you are angry, don't baby your grudge. Never go to sleep with anger in your heart, forgive quickly. If you steal, stop it. Use your hands for good. Give to those in need. Clean up your language. Speak only what is helpful and kind. Stop being mean and hateful. Never permit hate and prejudice to dwell in your mind."

The writer summarized all he wrote with a short practical prescription: "Be kind to each other, kindhearted, forgiving everyone, just as God has forgiven you, because you belong to my Son."

Kousin Zeke gave his own PRESCRIPTION FOR HAPPINESS. He sez, "Just use a smudge of Common Sense. Keep our faith up-to-date. Obey the Good Book. When we have the opportunity to do bad, don't. When we have the opportunity to do good, do it. If we halfway try this prescription, it will cut down on pills and doctor bills, and spread tons of joy to others and even us.

OUR GOOF-UPS

What can we do about our goof-ups? Another name for goof-up is sin. One major department store had such a problem trying to persuade people not to steal, that they put up a sign that read, "Stealing Is A Sin." They were hopeful the sign would discourage stealing. Many people become so deeply troubled about their goof-ups, they long for purity, peace and forgiveness. Their minds churn day and night, wondering if they will ever possess peace of mind and be free from their goof-ups. The guilt for many is so overwhelming that they take their own lives, never realizing that there is a solution, answer for their goof-ups. I'm thankful there is a way out. If I didn't know this I would not be writing this article. I would be searching high and low for a solution.

Kousin Zeke sez, "A writer wrote more than 5,000 years ago, God will forgive our sins and remove them as far as the East is from the West. For me, my wife and kids, that's all we wants to know." What does remove from the East to the West mean? When we travel from East to West, if we continue in that direction, we will always be going West. How far is that? It cannot be measured. What does that say to you and me? If we sincerely confess our goof-ups, change our direction, straighten up and fly right, God will faithfully forgive our goof-ups. This promise can heal broken hearts, broken lives and give peace of mind, and remove forever the guilt of our goof-ups (sins). This is HAPPINESS with a capital "H". A good habit, share what you have learned with a friend. (Read Psalm 103:1-12; 1 John 1:9).

℞ HE'S NO FOOL

Why would a person who was the chief executive officer (CEO) of H & R Block, the $1.7 billion tax preparation and financial-service firm, quit his position, to become a teacher at St. Francis Xavier middle school in Kansas City, Missouri? His annual salary suddenly dropped to less than $15,000 a year, about three percent of his old salary. That's what Tom Block did. He said, "The hardest part was telling my father," Henry Block, chairman of H & R Block, who co-founded the company in 1955.

The average Joe or Jane would consider Tom Block a fool, and would tell him, "Why would you make such a stupid decision?" Most of us are driving ourselves crazy, chasing life and success in frantic circles, trying to get where he was, where he is, and get what he had.

I'm going to let Tom Block tell you why he quit the rat race, "My hectic schedule as CEO had been interfering with my top priority, my wife and two sons. I didn't want to look back on my life and say, 'Gee, you had an opportunity to play a bigger role in your children's lives and you didn't do it.'"

I don't know about you, but it would do most of us good to do what Kousin Zeke sez, "Step back, take a peek and see where we is and where we is going. The way I looks at the world, an honest inventory, and look back for most of us could help to get our priorities on the right road." You and I must choose which juncture of the road we wish to travel. Tom Block chose not to miss his opportunity to help his family and others. He chose to use a PRESCRIPTION FOR HAPPINESS. Just be certain, "You and I know WHERE WE IS and WHERE WE IS GOING."

℞ THEY ARE NOT LOST

In the comic strip Dennis the Menace, cartoonist Hank Ketcham teaches his readers a fact of life necessary for peace of mind. The first scene shows Dennis sitting on a park bench with his mother and a friend, Mrs. Lewis. Dennis says, "How come we're sitting here?" His mother says, "Dennis – Please!" Her friend was upset and said, "I just lost my dad." Dennis replied, "Didn't you just say you lost your dad?" Mrs. Lewis says, "Yes, I did say that but..." "Well, let's go. I'll help ya look!" Dennis responded. Mrs. Lewis said, "But I didn't lose him in the park." "Then where did you lose him?" asked Dennis. "In the hospital," Mrs. Lewis replied sadly.

Dennis' mother called him over and began to whisper in his ear. Then Dennis said, "Ooohh! Well, why didn't you say so?" Dennis then said to Mrs. Lewis, "You didn't lose your dad, God took him! And when God takes somebody they're not lost! They're okay 'cuz they're with God! Do you understand Mrs. Lewis?" She replied, "I do now, Dennis."

That is a priceless lesson to learn and know. Dennis hit the nail on the head. We become so caught up with the fashion of this world and its things and junk that we won't be prepared for God's call when our number pops up. It will. Two facts of life we cannot avoid: Death and Taxes. There is a road map and compass for life's direction – God's Word. Read, study and obey it. Otherwise you may have to call on Dennis to explain God's plan to you.

Kousin Zeke sez, "A friend told me he shor had plenty of time and he was going to eat, drink and make merry and not worry 'bout his Christian faith until the clock hit 11:59. I tell's him, You shor gonna miss lots of fun, and what are you gonna do when your number pops up BEFORE 11:59?

[1] From HAPPY THOUGHTS TO KEEP AND GIVE AWAY by Jack C. Kelley

℞ WHAT'S YOUR DEFINITION OF HAPPINESS?

You may not know it, but every Tom, Dick, Harry and Jane is attempting to hard sell you their definition of happiness, like it or not. You are usually brainwashed in this manner:

- You've Come A Long Way Baby
- Diet Secrets That Work
- Win Millions With Lotto
- The Ultimate Pleasure
- 50% Off
- This Bud's For You
- Xmas in July

The choicest definition I've heard, "Happiness is not the absence of conflict but the ability to cope with it." Until we learn how to cope with life's struggles, living can become "tough sledding" and much "easier said than done". But it is very possible to be a content and happy person; it is up to each of us within ourselves. If we lack contentment, we need to examine our own thinking and attitudes.

A magazine gave five rules for happiness. I've adapted them somewhat:

1. Always look on the brighter side of life.
2. Accept cheerfully the place in life that is yours and live it to the fullest.
3. Put your soul and spirit into your work and give it your best.
4. Get into the habit of doing kindness and courtesies for others.
5. Adopt and maintain a simple childlike attitude of confidence and trust in God and Jesus.

Living by these rules can only comfort and help if we even halfway attempt to live and abide by them. LET S TRY!!!

[1] From HAPPY THOUGHTS TO KEEP AND GIVE AWAY by Jack C. Kelley

"Enthusiasm"
– Do You Have It? –

A so-called inspirational speaker was attempting to inspire some people to a higher level of enthusiasm. He said in a slow drawling voice "What ---we---need---is---more---en--thu-si---asm." He thought he had enthusiasm, but like lots of folks he don't have none. According to Emerson, "Nothing great was ever achieved without enthusiasm." I would like to quote an article by Erich Weiss about enthusiasm. "Knowledge is essential--but knowledge without enthusiasm is like a tire without air…like a bed without sheets…like a 'thank you' without a smile. Remove enthusiasm from worship service on Sunday and you have the making of a memorial service at a mortuary on a Monday."

Mr Weiss wrote, "When the odds are against us, the hours long, and the end is not yet in view, enthusiasm rescues us from the temptation to quit--or run away--or complain. It takes the grit and grind out of boredom. Athletes feed on it. Salesmen are motivated by it. Teachers count on it. Students fail without it. Leadership demands it." God's work succeeds with it. A story was told of two men in a military prison. One was sad and depressed. the other was quite happy. The sad soldier lamented that he had gone AWOL, and was in for thirty days. His smiling companion replied that he had murdered a general and was in for only three days. Astonished, the gloomy GI complained, "That isn't fair! Your crime was far more serious. Why am I in for thirty days--and you for only three?" Still smiling, the other GI answered. "They're going to hang me on Wednesday." The difference? ENTHUSIASM. Do you got it? If not get it.

COPING WITH AGITATORS[1]

Do you know, work with, or have contact with someone who bugs you, is a constant source of irritation and literally drives you up a wall? Joyce Landorf calls these people IRREGULAR PERSONS. I call them AGITATORS. Joyce says, "These people are the ones who have the knack of wounding you every time you see them. They make thoughtless remarks, ruin your day, and keep your emotions in constant turmoil. These people have negative personalities. You can't reason, depend or expect any support from them." You can expect criticism and fault-finding. Someone said, "An agitator can see more shortcomings through a keyhole than most through an open door." They can see the worst and best. Agitators are in every walk of life. You will find them where you work, play and live. Like it or not, you have to endure, tolerate, and live with them, unless you crawl into a ground-hog hole. I've seen the time when I would prefer to be in the hole with the ground-hog! The problem is how to cope, survive and learn to live with Agitators. It ain't easy. It takes all the patience, love and forgiveness you can stockpile.

A suggestion for coping with an agitator is to try to understand why he or she behaves in such a detestable manner. Some never improve, and as the farmer says, "they gets worser." Remember, you are not their only dartboard, they usually treat others the same way. You must alter your attitude and not permit them to control or dominate you. A word of caution – beware of anger! Anger is a virus that affects the attitude and spirit. Don't make hateful and harsh remarks. Always keep your relationships with others and God open, and your forgiveness up-to-date. Don't forget, you have two holes in your head, GARBAGE IN and GARBAGE OUT. You must choose to free your mind of negative garbage.

The choice is yours.

As difficult as it is, love and pray for the Agitator

[1] From HAPPY THOUGHTS TO KEEP AND GIVE AWAY by Jack C. Kelley

ANXIETY[1]

A lady overwhelmed by anxiety said, "I feel like I'm running from a dark cloud." Someone else said, "I'm boxed in and can't get out." Have you ever been there? Possibly you are there now. Anxiety may not kill you, but you might wish you were dead. A national clinic reported that anxiety is the number one emotional problem in America. One in ten men and one in five women will have a problem with anxiety. Left uncontrolled it can ruin lives, families, careers, marriages and friendships.

Anxiety is characterized by useless worry, fear, anger, hate, scary thoughts, mood swings, panic attacks, depression, feeling alone, hopelessness, guilty feelings, and an inability to eat or sleep. Often a chance incident can create a situation where we cannot cope or even make trivial decisions. How is it possible to win out, feel better, prevent crises from becoming anxieties? Here are some suggestions:

1. Realize we will look and feel better when we conquer our anxieties.
2. Think about the good side of life and forget the bad.
3. Stop dwelling on the past, it's finished – done and gone.
4. Try God's way. He understands our needs. That's the reason He sent Jesus, to give us peace.
5. Never forget, drugs and alcohol are not a solution.
6. Be thankful and decide you want to be someone others want to be with and around.

Share your blessings with someone who is hurting.
Now That's some Good Thinking!!!

[1] From HAPPY THOUGHTS TO KEEP AND GIVE AWAY by Jack C. Kelley

℞ HAPPINESS IS A CHOICE[1]

Did you ever wonder why some people are happy and some miserable, some sad and some glad, some have a smile and others have a frown? Believe it or not, happiness is a choice. A dear Quaker lady was asked to explain her obviously youthful appearance, her appealing vivacity and winning manner. She replied sweetly, "I use for the lips – TRUTH, for the voice – PRAYERS, for the eyes – PITY, for the hands – CHARITY, for the figure – UPRIGHTNESS, for the heart – LOVE." How's that for a facial makeup kit?

A friend told me that bitterness, anger, and hate all leave their mark on our face in the form of wrinkles. Bitterness is especially easy to see on a person's face. Remember, it takes less muscles to smile! There is not one of us that doesn't look better with a smile.

A large billboard on a major street in Tampa, Florida read, "HATE and RAGE are four letter words, but so are LOVE and HOPE. Hey, you got a choice." You can choose hate, envy, lust, bitterness, jealousy, selfishness, and complaining OR you can choose love, joy, peace, patience, kindness, goodness, gentleness and self-control. One fact is certain, if you make the right choices, your family and friends will be happier and maybe your dog won't bark and howl so much. Trust me, you'll look better with a smile.

[1] From HAPPY THOUGHTS TO KEEP AND GIVE AWAY by Jack C. Kelley

℞ Record Your Prescriptions For Happiness

℞ Record Your Presciptions For Happiness